COMMUNITY
Before SELF

MALIN BURNHAM

COMMUNITY
Before SELF

SEVENTY YEARS *of* MAKING WAVES

WITH MICHAEL S. MALONE

Advantage®

To Roberta, John, Cathe, Tom, and MaryBeth.
I could not have done all of this without you.

To Michael S. Malone,
thank you for breathing life into my story.

ACKNOWLEDGMENT

Atiya Davidson and Joe DiNucci
of EnablingThoughtLeadership.com

Thank you for starting and bringing this project to fruition.
Your team made my book a reality.

Published by Advantage, Charleston, South Carolina.
Member of Advantage Media Group.

ADVANTAGE is a registered trademark and the Advantage colophon is a trademark of Advantage Media Group, Inc.

Printed in the United States of America.

ISBN: 978-1-59932-736-5
LCCN: 2016932217

10 9 8 7 6 5 4 3 2

Book design by Matthew Morse.

This publication is designed to provide accurate and authoritative information in regard to the subject matter covered. It is sold with the understanding that the publisher is not engaged in rendering legal, accounting, or other professional services. If legal advice or other expert assistance is required, the services of a competent professional person should be sought.

Advantage Media Group is proud to be a part of the Tree Neutral® program. Tree Neutral offsets the number of trees consumed in the production and printing of this book by taking proactive steps such as planting trees in direct proportion to the number of trees used to print books. To learn more about Tree Neutral, please visit **www.treeneutral.com**. To learn more about Advantage's commitment to being a responsible steward of the environment, please visit **www.advantagefamily.com/green**

Advantage Media Group is a publisher of business, self-improvement, and professional development books and online learning. We help entrepreneurs, business leaders, and professionals share their Stories, Passion, and Knowledge to help others Learn & Grow. Do you have a manuscript or book idea that you would like us to consider for publishing? Please visit **advantagefamily.com** or call **1.866.775.1696**.

CONTENTS

FOREWORD

In the pages that follow, you are going to learn a lot about an extraordinary man: Malin Burnham. But what you aren't going to read about Malin is the singular role he plays in the lives of those who encounter him.

At a certain age, most of us lose our living role models. Ironically, if we are in any way successful in our own lives, we become mentors for others even as we are forced to proceed without anyone to personally guide us through our aging process.

Luckily, in Malin Burnham, many of us on the threshold of retirement are blessed to have found the person we'd like to be in our later years. At eighty-eight, Malin has more energy, is more engaged in his community, is more effective at getting things done, and is happier than the vast majority of people we meet. You cannot help but watch Malin in action and not say to yourself: "I only hope I can be half as vital as that man at his age."

I first met Malin Burnham when I became president of Stanford University. He, of course, was already a legend on campus—an alumnus long known as "Mr. Stanford in San Diego." I soon learned that, over the previous half century,

Malin had served on three of the most important boards at Stanford (the athletic department, the alumni association, and ultimately, the board of trustees); that he had supported the refurbishment of the Stanford Pavilion (now called the Burnham Pavilion), which today houses gymnastics, volleyball, and wrestling competitions; and that he had established a permanent scholarship in our engineering department.

For those efforts and more, Malin had received several of Stanford's highest honors, including induction as the third member in the Stanford Professionals in Real Estate Hall of Fame and the highest award for exceptional volunteer service, the Gold Spike.

All of that was impressive enough, but when I got to know him, I discovered that his Stanford activities were in addition to all he had done for his hometown of San Diego. There are few philanthropists in American history who have contributed to their cities in more ways than Malin has to San Diego. You can stand on almost any corner in downtown San Diego, look in almost any direction, and see Malin Burnham's handiwork. Most of these transformations do not bear Malin's name, because that's the way he is. When his name does appear over the entrance of a building, it is usually last in order—because, like a few great leaders, Malin knows that getting the job done is more important than getting the credit.

And "gets the job done" describes Malin Burnham better than any phrase I know. It is one of the reasons people admire him so. As far back as the America's Cup competitions and as recently as his work in stem-cell research, Malin has shown an ability to turn visions into reality. He is almost fearless: he thinks big (consider the giant aircraft carrier USS *Midway*, now berthed in San Diego) and takes joy in asking people to give of their treasure for causes that are truly compelling. He also seems to have an instinctive understanding of when he should advise a charity, when he should sit on its board, when he should chair, and when he should leave.

These are just some of the reasons why Malin Burnham is so special and why we at Stanford University—and most assuredly his neighbors in San Diego—prize the man so highly. He has lived a remarkable life. He has accomplished extraordinary things. He is beloved by those who have known him and will leave this world a far better place than he found it. And he lives his life with energy and enthusiasm, certainly contributing to his own happiness.

His success has led many younger people to examine their own lives and consider how they could emulate Malin's achievements. What has been missing over the years, however, is the recipe: a detailed description by Malin about how and why he does what he does and why his life has been such a consistent trail of success.

Now, with this book, Malin has given us a wonderful valedictory gift. It is less an autobiography than the accumulated wisdom of nearly nine decades; it is less a personal memoir than a guide to current and future philanthropists on how to convert their success in the commercial world to even greater success in nonprofits. But most of all, it is priceless advice from a great man on how to live a happy and rewarding life in public and private.

This is the book many have been waiting for, and I predict that the people around the world who read this book assiduously will return to it often. It is a guidebook for the rest of all our lives.

John Hennessy
President, Stanford University

INTRODUCTION

As I entered full time into the nonprofit world in 1987, I realized that I needed to reorient some of my thinking, especially my priorities. Yes, I was interested in helping to make the greater San Diego region a better place to live, work, and play. But how?

As the next few years rolled by, it became clearer that the best way to achieve my objectives was to employ more teamwork in my endeavors. Soon I came upon my motto: "Community before self." I began describing community as family, neighborhood, city, county, state, and country. But it is also much more, such as partners, owners, teammates, customers, and charity recipients.

To further identify my theme, I printed up a supply of "Community before self" cards that I hand out to small groups on occasions when I believe a focus needs to be adopted. I was very careful to not put my name on the cards, because I truly believe that community comes before self.

Hopefully, the above explanation takes away any mystery about the title of this book. What follows are some of my experiences using this theme as my beacon.

CHAPTER 1

PIVOT POINTS

There are a lot of days and a lot of events in the course of a lifetime, especially one as long as mine. When you look back, most of those days and events are a lot like each other: baby steps forward or backward along an endless path.

But some days and some events—and especially the decisions and choices you make on those eventful days—stand above the rest as being profoundly more important. These are the *pivot points* in one's life: the decisions made or not made; the choices, big but often seemingly inconsequential, that turn out to have changed the entire direction of your life. It is at these pivot points that the narrative of your life can turn for the better or the worse. They can open doors to great opportunities, or they can close doors. They can lead to life experiences you either celebrate or forever regret.

Looking back, it is easy to see these pivot points—they tower like mountains over the foothills of the rest of one's lived days. They are so obvious that you are astounded by how you ever missed seeing them for what they were at the time.

And there's the problem. Pivot points can be easy to see in the rearview mirror, but they are mostly invisible through the windshield. There's no sign pointing at a fork in the road, no line in a business letter, no pretty face saying, "follow/read/choose *this,* and your life will change forever."

It just isn't in the realm of human ability to identify all these pivot points, but it is possible to learn to be better at discerning them as you approach them. And it is possible to recognize the change before you've gone too far down a new path and make the best of the new reality in which you find yourself. Sometimes, as we'll see, a seemingly wrong choice can turn out to be a good one (and vice versa).

Sometimes, if you are lucky, you can even make your own pivot point—though always beware of getting what you wished for...

• • •

The first great pivot point in my life was one I made at the beginning of my junior year at Stanford University.

I'd returned home from winning a sailing championship, intent on joining the Navy, when I learned that my father had arranged my entrance into Stanford. When I arrived in Palo Alto that September, I had no idea what career I wanted to follow, so I chose engineering because my best subjects in high school were math and physics.

My choice to pursue engineering pleased my father, who quickly began imagining my future as the CEO of Westinghouse or General Motors. I didn't have the heart to tell him that engineering was far from my first love or that I had no interest in a corporate career.

At the beginning of my junior year, when it was required to choose which engineering discipline would become my major degree, my views hadn't changed. I had done well enough as an engineering student, but I had also come to believe that my destiny was in San Diego and joining my father's real estate, mortgage, and insurance brokerage business. My decision was complicated: I was not deciding which engineering career held the most promise but rather which engineering discipline had the most useful stuff that I could cannibalize for a very different career path.

Today, a counselor would probably have suggested that I "follow my dream" and switch to a business or finance major, but that notion only briefly crossed my mind before I dismissed it. I've never regretted doing so.

In the end, I chose to major in industrial engineering. It taught me important lessons about accounting, finance, marketing, and law. Sure, I probably could have cobbled those subjects together in the business school, but I doubt I could have found in business the *really* valuable lessons of my industrial engineering degree: practicality versus theory, results versus strategies, and most of all, rigorous and empirical analysis. Engineering school taught me how to analyze people, arguments, building designs, financing plans, political power, and more. Looking back, it was the best possible education for the career that followed.

My choice of major was a pivot point I didn't recognize at the time—and not for many years. But what I did do right at the time was to not look back or have any regrets. From the day I joined my father's company, I never again wondered what my life would have been like if I had become an engineer.

• • •

The most terrifying pivot points are those you take blindly.

In 1982, I was invited to join the board of the La Jolla Cancer Research Foundation (LJCRF), a young medical research institute in La Jolla that was dedicated to discovering the fundamental molecular causes of disease and developing therapies based on those discoveries. I knew nothing about the science of cancer diagnosis or treatment—happily, there had been no cancer in my extended family—so I hesitated to make a commitment.

Then the La Jolla folks said something interesting to me. They told me that everyone who worked there lived in La Jolla—not just the scientists but also the members of the board, the accountant, the attorney, and everyone else. This struck me oddly; somehow the information seemed crucially important. So I agreed to visit, even though I had always been a thoroughly downtown San Diego kind of guy.

What they showed me turned out to be yet another pivot point.

I had always assumed that research science, especially in medicine, was conducted by individual scientists, each working in a vacuum and separated from their peers so that valuable discoveries and secrets could not be stolen.

What I saw at the LJCRF (later the Burnham Institute) was just the opposite. It was all about families, networks, and partners. It was seven years before I finally understood the right word for it: *collaboration.* Then and now, LJCRF had collaboration deeper in its DNA than I have ever seen. I agreed to join as a trustee.

It proved to be a crucial pivot point. For one thing, my hunch proved correct. The same collaborative culture that thrilled me on my first visit has enabled the institute to move to the forefront of cancer research. Just as important, being engaged at the LJCRF taught me important things about the power of collaboration, which I have tried to put to use in the other organizations with which I have been involved.

• • •

In the early 1980s, the San Diego Olympic Foundation was formed to compete with other US cities to build an all-weather, all-year training center for the United States Olympic Committee (USOC). It faced considerable competition from New York City, which fielded its own committee—led by the redoubtable owner of the Yankees, George Steinbrenner.

I agreed to be chair of the building committee, and I was scheduled to appear before the thirty-person board of the USOC to present San Diego's proposal. I knew we had a good case; what I didn't expect was that our entire case would ultimately revolve around *me.*

After some forty-five minutes of my slide show and a Q&A session, the board raised the one question I hadn't anticipated: How could the USOC be confident that once it started, the San Diego Olympic Foundation would finish this substantial project?

I took a very deep breath, pivoted to my own past, and said, "Of all the real estate projects I've ever started, I've never failed to finish one." I didn't pause to think that I had just put my own reputation on the line with one of the nation's most influential private institutions.

There was no further discussion. The board voted its approval of the San Diego facility, and the rest is history.

• • •

Sometimes your biggest pivot points come when you help others deal with theirs.

In 1996, fourteen years after being on the board, the LJCRF was kind enough to rename itself the Burnham Institute. In 2007 the name was changed to the Sanford Burnham Institute. Today it is the Sanford Burnham Prebys Medical Discovery Institute. Therein lies a tale, one that revolves around that first name in the title.

T. Denny Sanford is a remarkable individual. He was born in Minnesota, attended the University of Minnesota, and started a distribution company at a young age. He made a fortune with that company, sold it, and then embarked on a career of doing interesting and progressive new things.

Denny bought a bank in Sioux Falls about twenty years ago. He fixed it up, got bored, and was ready to sell it when a friend told him that with South Dakota changing its usury law, he should turn the bank into a credit card company. Denny listened—and the resulting company turned into a multibillion enterprise.

Denny Sanford and I met in the most unlikely of circumstances. On a World Presidents' Organization charter flight around the world in 2007, he hit it off with a friend of mine. Denny had just made his first big philanthropic gift of $400 million to a South Dakota hospital group. Learning that, my friend said, "Hey, I'm on the board of the Burnham Institute in San Diego. Why don't you come out for my sixty-fifth birthday and see the place?"

He agreed, and I met Denny Sanford for the first time.

Denny obviously enjoyed the party and the tour because three weeks later, he came back to San Diego with two of his people for a second, deeper look. At its end, we sat in a conference room and talked. He told us that his current interest was in pediatric healthcare. We replied that we had a number of grants in pediatric research but had never combined them. That's when Denny had his own pivot point. He asked us to go to the blackboard. "Can you write it up?"

We did as he asked, and the result was a $20 million gift to start a pediatric research center at the institute.

That was just the beginning. Californians approved a proposition in 2004 for a $3 billion bond issue to underwrite stem-cell research. Over a ten-year period, there would be other pivot points to come. We created a task force to discuss how to combine the four great medical research facilities in La Jolla—University of California, San Diego (UCSD); Salk; Scripps; and Burnham—into a consortium to pursue this research money. The state stipulated that any such building grant would have to be matched in part by a gift.

South Dakota had already voted down such research, so it was the perfect moment to go back to Denny. I told him we needed a $10 million gift and that in exchange he would get his name on the building.

Well, I'm not a very good poker player. Denny came back to me and said that for that money he should get his name on the entire consortium. I told him we already had a guy in Los Angeles willing to give $30 million for the same thing, but he had made a couple stipulations we didn't want.

Denny finally came back and agreed: $10 million up front and $20 million over the next ten years. With his money, we built a spectacular new four-story, 130,000-square-foot stem-cell research laboratory that had no equal in the world.

Next, we quietly put together a campaign for $100 million to expand the operations of the Burnham Institute. Denny heard about that, too—he said he'd put up the first $50 million if we'd get the next $50 million—and of course he wanted his name on it. I could hardly say no, even if I had to surrender the position of my name.

So I went to him and asked, "How should we decide which name comes first?" I suggested we flip a coin. Denny agreed, but "only if we use my two-headed coin." That's when he made the decisive point: there was no way he was going to put his money into something destined to be called the "BS Institute." At least that's how he tells the story. I'm not going to argue. Denny's money proved transformative to the institute.

Even after these remarkable gifts, Denny still wasn't finished. Five years later, UCSD decided that it wanted to build its own on-campus stem-cell clinic. Denny agreed to put up $100 million.

So thanks to a chance meeting on a plane and a spontaneous invitation to a birthday party, followed by one opportunity after another to help a remarkable man find some pivot points of his own, medical research in San Diego was transformed. Today there is the Sanford Burnham Prebys Medical Discovery Institute, the Sanford Consortium for Regenerative Medicine, and the Sanford Stem Cell Clinical Center at UC San Diego.

As for me, I found my own pivot point in all of this. I learned that if you care more about results than ego, sometimes the smartest thing to do is get out of the way and share credit with others. If I had refused Denny's initial request to put his name first, some of these subsequent miracles might not have happened—and many patients would likely not be alive today.

• • •

Different people, even when encountering the same opportunity, have different pivot points.

Take that third name on the title of the Discovery Institute: Conrad Prebys. Conrad came to San Diego forty years ago with $500 in his pocket, no job, and no car. He got into construction and then apartment real estate. Fast forward to today, and he owns seven thousand apartment units in the San Diego area. He is a marvelous person and is deeply committed to the local arts community.

I first met Conrad thirty years ago when I was still in the banking world, and over the years I have come to know him well. He's a good friend. In 2009, he put up $10 million to create the Conrad Prebys Center for Chemical Genomics at the Burnham Institute. It was a very timely contribution. We'd just received a grant from the National Institutes of Health to acquire several large robotic machines—the best in the world—capable of identifying as many as *one million* chemical compounds per day. This not only served our internal needs but also enabled us to take on contract work for revenue.

I bring up Conrad because of the difference in the way he gives compared to Denny. In Conrad's case, the initial introduction to an opportunity has got to grab him by the gut; it must be an epiphany. That is his pivot point. He doesn't necessarily commit immediately, but that's how he gets initially engaged. He'll research the opportunity, calculate the right commitment, and then make his move. But if it isn't love at first sight, it's very rare that he will ever make a gift. His pivot point is in that first moment, so you'd better put your very best foot forward in that first encounter.

Denny, by comparison—more than any other philan-thropist I know—looks around and spots needs, especially in health and education, and he often makes the initial contact. He creates his own first pivot point, and it is up to you to present him with subsequent opportunities.

• • •

While each of these pivot points were important, the biggest pivot in my life was my decision to retire early. But it was the way I chose to deal with the aftermath of retirement that proved to be my finest decision.

Most successful people retire one of two ways:

They don't. Their life is their work, and they have done very well at it. They are not nearly so good at anything else. So why retire at all? Why not die in harness? Frankly, many of these folks are secretly convinced that as long as they are working, they can't die. Many also believe that their creation can't long outlive them, and they don't want to sit idle and frustrated, watching their life's work disintegrate.

They become retirees. They take the term "retirement" too seriously, walking away from their former busy life to nothing in particular beyond a vague notion of "taking it easy." Inevita-bly, these once-active people soon grow bored with their new static existence and drift back into action. But they've wasted time and momentum, they've grown older, and by the time they get back rolling again, they have little time left and, more often than not, no real plan.

That's why I think I made the right decision by creating my own pivot point. I've now been "retired" as long as I "worked" in my career. I had gone as far as I wanted to in my business life and had accomplished just about everything I set out to do. Perhaps I could have achieved even more over the last three decades if I had stayed in place, but at best it still wouldn't have been as meaningful as what has been accomplished by my pivot into the world of philanthropy.

Furthermore—and of course I can't say this with certainty—I believe that I've lived longer and continued to make a contribution longer precisely because I made the jump early, settled into my new life quickly, and never became a retiree. In fact, if you were to see my daily work life today, it would not look very different from my business days back when I was running my company. I still maintain a fifty-hour weekly schedule with a full-time assistant at a central downtown office. I have a daily stretching and exercise routine, and my wife Roberta continues to orchestrate our social and travel activities. In my late eighties, I am still as engaged and vital as ever. Surely genes and luck have something to do with this, but I also can't help believing that I wouldn't be in my current, happy state if I had stayed on the job or gone home to rust.

• • •

Looking back, every important period in my life has been the product of successfully navigating through a pivot point, either one I saw coming or one that caught me by surprise. Pivot points truly are game changers. They determine your destiny—whether it will be happy or sad, satisfying or frustrating, a success or a failure.

In the best of all worlds, you create your pivot points and manage your path through them. Second best is to identify one coming and stay the course. But even when a pivot point catches you by surprise, if you can just stay on top of the process, you increase the odds of having a good conclusion.

As that great philosopher Yogi Berra said: "When you come to a fork in the road, *take it!*"

CHAPTER 2

START EARLY

Too many people save their most important good works until the very end of their lives. There are a lot of reasons for this. It may be that they are too busy with their careers to take on the added responsibilities of charitable work. Or they are raising children. Or they want to wait until they have enough money to make a real impact. Or, I'm convinced, they wait because they think they are supposed to wait because philanthropy is the work of one's old age.

I believe that this attitude is wrong for many reasons. For one thing, you have more energy early in your working life. Sure, you're busy—but in my experience, you aren't much less busy in retirement. Those same traits that made you successful in your career are guaranteed to fill up your calendar in retirement. In addition, in the middle of your career, you are more in the thick of things; you have more influence, connections, and social power. In retirement, many of those connections begin to fade as those contacts themselves retire or are promoted out of day-to-day operations into more advisory and ceremonial roles.

But most important, many projects may take years to realize, and if you wait until you are old to initiate them, you may run out of time to see them to their completion. That will not only cost you the satisfaction of seeing the culmination of some of your life's most important work, but can you truly be sure that this work will *ever* get done?

Look around you and see how many legacy programs, no matter how carefully designed, staffed, and funded, fall apart or go off in a tangential direction—or worst of all, get subverted and do exactly the opposite of what their creators designed them to do. The best strategy, then, for guaranteeing that your vision is followed for decades and perhaps even gets fulfilled, is to start early—and if possible, to live long.

• • •

I've always been a person who starts early. It's better to be the guy who is always ten minutes early to a meeting than to be the guy who is ten minutes late. You can credit this to acquired discipline, but in fact, I must've been born this way.

That said, there have been two forces in my life that have amplified this sense of needing to always be early, and they in turn have taught me the advantages of this attitude as a strategy for life.

The first was competitiveness, itself the product of confidence. I can remember, at the age of ten in the mid-1930s, my mother would take my older brother and me down to the beach in San Diego in the summer. I watched enraptured as the little sailboats—sixteen-foot Junior-class boats—went back and forth in the water. I dreamed of being out there piloting my own sailboat. But there was no sailing in my family; my father was an avid golfer, instead.

One day a miracle occurred: one of the boats sailed close, and the young pilot shouted out to my brother and me, "Hey, want to go sailing?" I couldn't get out on the water fast enough. My folks, bless them, saw my enthusiasm and took out a family membership in the San Diego Yacht Club. Soon my brother and I had signed up for sailing class. Our instructor taught us about boating, sailing, safety, and maintenance. On the weekends we were allowed to compete in two-person crews, with the skipper and crew member swapping places between Saturday and Sunday.

My brother enjoyed the experience; I *loved* it. Looking back, the real breakthrough occurred during the summer of my thirteenth year. That summer, I surpassed my brother, whose interests were starting to drift away. I, on the other hand, became even more obsessed with sailing and ever more confident in my skills. There was a good reason for this: when you are sailing and are out there on the water, there is no guarantee that you will return. You have no motor, and getting back to the dock is utterly dependent upon your skill with sail and tiller. Once you've succeeded at that task twenty or thirty times, you have complete confidence that you will always be able to sail home. That's a very big deal for a thirteen-year-old boy. It's a belief in one's own abilities that you carry throughout your life.

Now confident that I was as good as any other young sailor out there, I became more competitive and began winning races against older boys. When I turned fifteen and graduated out of the Junior Starlet class level into the Star class, my parents bought me my own Star sailboat: twenty-two feet long and the most popular class in international competition. It would be the class I would sail and compete in for the next thirty-five years. I would be on my own; my brother, at this point, had been lured away by cars and horses. But sailing, I knew, was my destiny. I got my own crewman, and though I knew nothing about leadership theory, I had the confidence—and apparently, the aptitude—to be a real skipper. Even though we were often the youngest Star sailors out there, we won more than our share of races.

August 1945 saw the Star World Championship held in Stamford, Connecticut, and I resolved to go. It was a different era then; my parents barely thought twice about letting me go. I was seventeen years old and had just graduated from high school, and my crewman, Lowell North, was just fifteen. We took the train back east, competed in the week-long regatta, and astonishingly, *we won!* It turned out to be an historic achievement. At seventeen I was, and still remain, the youngest ever Star World Champion skipper.

Me (second row, second from the right) and the rest of my
high school's Senior Boys Club.

Needless to say, it was a celebratory trip home—in more ways than one. I can remember the train stopping, unscheduled, somewhere in Kansas. The word had arrived that the Japanese had surrendered. It was V-J Day; World War II was over. We partied for an hour and then continued on our way.

My parents came up from San Diego to meet us at Union Station in Los Angeles. On the way home we had time to talk about the championship and my plans for the future. I told my dad that, like my older friends, I wanted to join the Navy, but my father vetoed the idea. No, he said, the war's over; everyone's coming home. There's no future in the military. Instead, he told me, he'd talked to a friend of his in the insurance business and had arranged an opportunity for me to attend Stanford University.

In retrospect, my father was both right and timely. Getting into Stanford that September put me into college just before the tidal wave of returning veterans on the GI Bill swamped the nation's universities, filling every slot. Had I waited a year, I never would have been able to enroll at Stanford—or possibly anywhere else.

Because math and physics were my best subjects in high school, I chose engineering as my major. As time went on, I began to lose interest in it. In 1947, at the beginning of my junior year (when I had to commit to my engineering major), I realized that what I really wanted to do after graduation was go back to San Diego and work with my father. So at a time when most of my classmates were pursuing "jobs of the future" and jumping into aeronautical or electrical engineering, I chose industrial engineering, not least because it required me to take courses in law, accounting, and marketing. It was a decision I've never regretted.

Two years later, I was twenty-one years old, and my characteristic early starts—unrestrained by schedules and age limits—came to the fore. I graduated in the summer of 1949. Within a week, I was back in San Diego and working at my father's real estate and insurance company, where I stayed my entire career.

I was also about to get married. I had met Chatter in high school, and we'd managed to maintain a long-distance relationship. Now that I was home, neither of us saw any reason to wait. We were married in August. We didn't wait on children, either; our twins, a boy and girl, were born nine months later. And we had two more children before I was twenty-seven. Chatter and I were married for twenty years before divorcing.

Younger readers may find such a life path to be most unusual—even bizarre. That's understandable: modern life and modern life expectancies argue for waiting a few years before embarking on adulthood. In the post-World War II world, this quick jump into adulthood was far more common, though it was still pretty rare to do so at twenty-one and then stick with it.

My brother chose a very different path. Whereas I have always believed in being part of a team, he was more independent, always choosing to go it alone. While I joined my father in his company, my brother went off and founded his own insurance company. He was very happy—showing that there is more than one path to an accomplished career.

· · ·

One might also look at my early decisions and see someone attracted to a "safe" life. In fact, I didn't see my choices as safe and conservative at all. On the contrary, getting married and becoming a father so early and working for my father was a strategy fraught with risk. I wasn't fearful; if anything I was overconfident. I knew what I wanted to do, and not seeing any reason to wait, I jumped in as early as possible. After all, I was going to live in San Diego for the rest of my life, I knew I had an aptitude for the real estate business, I knew whom I wanted to marry, and I knew that I wanted kids. So why sit around pondering it? Let's get started!

Having that kind of confidence and then acting on it only increased my confidence. Knowing that I could work well with my father freed me from worrying about all the small concerns of office politics and kept my focus on the larger picture: the expansion of the firm, developing networks in downtown San Diego, staffing, and our portfolio of services. I made myself vital to our company precisely because I knew I had a lifetime stake in it. I wasn't going anywhere; its success would be my success.

In my private life, because I wasn't perpetually moving and starting over at new jobs that demanded endless hours per week, I was able to focus on the other two things that mattered most to me: my family and sailing. I wanted to spend time with my wife and kids, and I wanted to go a long way in sailboat racing. Because of my manageable work schedule, I was able to really be there for my family and at the same time, go all the way to the America's Cup.

For the first few years, I kept my head down at work. Because I was going to be at the company for a very long time, I wanted to learn the business from the ground up. I didn't think about where the company was going, but instead, I spent all my time learning from employees senior to me about the nature and mechanics of insurance, mortgages, and residential and commercial real estate. I figured that if I was going to help lead my company into the future, then I should start by learning everything I could about its present.

One of the basic skills I learned during those early years was how to appraise a house with nothing more than a clipboard and a tape measure. And I appraised a lot of them, doing work by hand that is done today with laser measurers, digital cameras, laptops, and wireless access to appraisal databases in "the cloud." As a measure of how far we've come, I was doing all that handwork in the field for mortgages that—according to John Hancock Mutual Life Insurance Co., the biggest lender in the country—could not exceed $10,000. These days, the average mortgages on the same houses approach $1 million.

One of the biggest advantages of learning and doing the job by hand is that you end up with a more practical and realistic view of how much time and energy it takes for the work to get done. This proves hugely valuable when you begin to think about staffing.

During this period, our company grew rapidly. I like to think that it was because we provided superior service, but I readily admit that this was a period when the whole nation, particularly California and especially San Diego, was enjoying unprecedented growth and expansion thanks to all of those returning GIs getting married and raising families. The Korean War and the Cold War were also underway. San Diego Bay was again filling with warships and Navy personnel, and sailors and their officers needed homes, too.

Every company welcomes growth, but many don't know how to handle it. Because senior management doesn't really know the parameters of the work their employees are doing, they misestimate the real cost of doing business and hire either too many or too few new employees to support that growth. In the former case, they waste good profits, and in the latter, they deliver inferior service to their customers. Having been out there with my clipboard and tape measure, I had a very good idea of the real cost and productivity we should expect from each new hire, so we were able to grow almost without a hitch.

Working with my father during these years was an interesting experience. Being the first in my family to go to college, I knew he was proud of me—but he didn't coddle me. He was a serious businessman, and he was equally proud of the company he had built. He wasn't going to risk it by giving even more authority to me if I couldn't handle it. Over the course of the next decade, he was pleased to see that I could.

Looking back, the last big lesson my father taught me was the most important of all. When he turned sixty-two, he retired and promoted me—at just age thirty-two—to CEO of the company. He moved up to the position of chairman of the board. Just three years later, at age sixty-five, he retired from business altogether. His retirement came as something of a surprise to the company and even to me, though he'd been talking about it for some time. We never really believed he'd do it. But he had always been a man of his word, and this time was no different. As for me, I worried about what my dad would do with so much free time while he was still so young. He'd always been a hard-working man.

I shouldn't have worried. My father knew exactly what he was doing. He and my mother loved power boating—a secondary effect of their support for my sailing—and it wasn't long before the two of them were spending much of their time on the water, traveling with friends up and down the southern California coast and having a great time. It was a wonderful retirement and a lesson to me, which I quietly tucked away in the back of my mind for the next thirty years.

Now the company was mine to run—to succeed or fail. Compared to most of my CEO peers, I was quite young. But unlike most of them, I'd already been with the firm for a decade, holding every position on the organizational chart—another advantage of starting early. Most of the other CEOs were relatively new to their firms, had been hired from elsewhere, and had never spent a day in the field. My experience would be my competitive advantage.

I was already making changes. I'd always been conservative in my career choices, but ironically I was something of a radical in this phase of my career. Once again I started early. One of the most irritating features of the mortgage industry had been the irregular way in which it frequently changed the rules. For example, the biggest lender, John Hancock, would send us a list of rules that set out the parameters of mortgage loans. Then every nine or ten months, just about the time we had the new program fully underway, they would completely change those parameters for no obvious reason and force us to accept a new rulebook.

This seemingly arbitrary rule changing drove my father crazy, but he never did anything about it. I refused to accept the status quo. If we know that John Hancock is going to do this, I asked, why don't we change our business practices to *anticipate* their actions? My argument, and especially my confidence in making it, helped convince my father that I was up to the task of taking over the company.

The greatest challenge in my career as CEO of John Burnham & Company came in the late 1950s, right about the time I became CEO of the company. Once again, being early proved critical—this time, to our very survival.

During those years in the real estate world, the larger companies were beginning to grow in prominence as they embarked on strategies of national expansion. I began to hear rumors that many of these firms—Coldwell Banker was a good example—were planning to come to San Diego to establish branch offices.

My first reaction was despair: how could we survive a challenge coming from these giants? Once I calmed down, I came up with a strategy. The first step was to talk to all my professional contacts and confidantes in San Diego—contractors, lawyers, bankers, and brokers, all of them older than me and all of them prominent in the city. I asked every one of them the same question: *How can my company survive?*

Nearly every mentor said to me, "You've got to get out as a leader and know your community better than your competitors do. Get acquainted with and be knowledgeable about people in the business world and also with nonprofits and government people."

I took their advice with alacrity, getting to everyone on my target list before my competitors could. Once I got a foothold, my senior VP began to develop his network, as well. It wasn't long before I was spending a third of my time involved in community service and local government.

The strategy succeeded. By the time the "Big Boys" came to San Diego to set up their offices, we were well established at the highest levels of every part of my city's life. We got the contracts they didn't even know were available, and we often closed deals after board meetings or luncheons to which they weren't even invited. If this suggests that I was actually being selfish in my motives for this charitable work, I won't argue. But then, you also don't know the nature of nonprofit volunteer work: once you put a toe in, it isn't long before you find yourself in over your head. I happily found myself in this position. As the years passed, I found myself more and more engaged with these programs with no other purpose than to offer them my talents, money, and time.

In light of this volunteer work, I was once again early— this time in forming my own charitable organization. As I said,

I think it is a mistake for people to wait to become philan-thropic until the end of their lives. My wife and I were resolved not to make that mistake. So we created our foundation in 1981, while we were still in our early fifties. We didn't have much money to put into it, but after some success both with my business and our stock investments, we had enough to have some small impact on our interests. The amount of money didn't matter; it was a start, and it was training ground for us to learn how to conduct smart philanthropy without the wherewithal to make big mistakes.

• • •

Starting a foundation also did something else: it disciplined our thinking. By then we had long been giving annual donations to charity, but our giving was usually erratic. We gave a lot in good years and not so much in bad ones. By creating the foundation and fulfilling the IRS requirement of donating 5 percent per year, we gained both discipline and consistency. Our support for the community leveled and thus became more predictable and dependable for the recipients.

In those years, I made other "early" decisions. One of them had a powerful bearing on how we built our business. I had always known where I wanted to live and work: San Diego. Knowing that, I built a powerful base for the company and my own life there. Why have national ambitions for the company and risk losing what made our firm so effective? No, we would remain a regional company, build for quality over quantity, and be as strong a competitor as possible in our home market. I also realized that I had enough wealth; I had no desire to be a billionaire. Unlike many people I've met in business, I avoided the trap of always wanting twice what I had.

Most of all, I decided—years before most of my contemporaries—that I didn't want to make my work my life. I had other callings, and I wanted to leave enough time in my life to pursue them. So at the peak of my career, I decided to retire from it.

I realize that such a choice is not for everyone. A good friend of mine, a great guy who was a dozen years older than me, came to San Diego during World War II. He started his own company in 1946 and built it into a very successful enterprise. He ran that company until the day he died as founder, chairman, president, and CEO. It was his entire life. As I said, he was a great guy, and he seemed happy with his life choice, but I knew from an early age that his path wasn't for me.

• • •

Is starting early the key to a happy and successful life? I can only say that it was for me. As I've tried to show, there are other paths to a satisfying and eventful life. What I am prepared to say is that to be successful, it is important to have a serious life. Not a dour one but rather one in which you take what you are doing seriously and are deliberate about where you're going and where you intend to end up. And you need to be serious about leaving a positive mark on this world. The earlier you decide to be serious about those things, the better your odds are of being successful at achieving your goals … and at looking back on your life without regrets.

CHAPTER 3

MAKING WAVES

I am a devout believer in making waves. Why? Because I know of no better way of getting people's attention—and with that attention, making positive things happen.

And how do you make waves? In water and in life, you need to throw a well-placed rock.

Over the course of my long life, I've never made bigger waves—literally and metaphorically—than during my years with the America's Cup race. We did so by taking enormous risks: rethinking the very nature of maritime competition in front of millions of people around the world. As you can imagine, the potential for global humiliation haunted us every step of the way.

A major force on our America's Cup team was Dennis Conner. I have known Dennis Conner since he was a teenager in the late 1950s, long before he became a sailing legend. He was nineteen and I was thirty-four when we first sailed in competition together. It was a long-distance race—ten days from San Diego to Acapulco. What I remember most about that race was that Dennis was an irrepressible bundle of energy and curiosity. We joked that he never tied down a sheet (a rope attached to a sail) but just kept running around, constantly readjusting them to make the ship go faster. That was his obsession: wringing one more ounce of speed out of our craft.

So tenacious was young Conner, so unrelenting in his questions and suggestions, that we affectionately nicknamed him "SAK" for "smart-ass kid."

It is from such single-mindedness that champions are made. We would race on the weekends, and on Monday afternoons after he finished school, Dennis would sit on the steps of Ash Bown's house and talk to the veteran sailor about the previous race. He would debrief Ash on what had gone right and what had gone wrong and would listen intently to advice about how he could improve his performance. Dennis would pepper Ash with questions about turns, choices of sails, and all of the minutiae of competitive sailing—and he would remember everything the forty-five-year-old captain told him. Ash was amazingly patient as these Monday visits went on for almost three years.

This description of Dennis Conner might surprise some readers. After all, Dennis has a very different public reputation. But having known and worked with him now for more than a half century, I know that there are two Dennis Conners. On land he can be notoriously abrupt, impatient, and short on small talk. That's the Dennis the world knows.

On water, he is a wholly different person and one of the best team leaders I've ever seen. People love to sail with Dennis because he is well organized, never yells, is respectful of his crew, and is always asking for their input. Combine those traits with decades of competing at the highest levels in the sport and an encyclopedic mind for facts and figures, and you begin to understand why Dennis Conner is one of the best sailors of the modern era.

Needless to say, given his potential, I religiously followed Dennis's career as he developed into adulthood and his reputation grew. Having been a sailing champion myself, I instinctively knew that he had what it took to go all the way—perhaps even to the biggest race of them all, the America's Cup. So I watched with pride and pleasure for the hometown boy as he won an Olympic Bronze in 1976 as well as multiple world championships throughout the decade. It all peaked in 1980, when he and his team successfully defended the Cup.

Then disaster struck. If you were around in 1983, you'll remember the headlines, which reverberated around the world: after 132 years of successfully defending the America's Cup, the New York Yacht Club (NYYC)—represented by a boat skippered by Dennis Conner—lost to a team from Australia.

As you can imagine, it was a devastating loss—and not least for Dennis. Anyone of lesser character might have gone away to hide from the blame and bad publicity. But not Dennis Conner; he redoubled his efforts to win back the Cup. And it wasn't long before much of the rest of the sailing world began to take his side—especially once photographs appeared of the winning Australian boat and its radically new keel.

Going into the 1983 race, our team had followed the traditional strategy of incrementally improving our competitiveness. This was done by having two nearly identical boats racing each other, with one remaining untouched and serving as the baseline "control" boat and the other as the "research" boat on which experimental changes were made one at a time.

But when we saw the Australian boat with its radically new "upside down" (wider at the bottom than the top) keel featuring a pair of projecting triangular "wings"—the idea being to reduce surface drag by reducing the size of the capillary bubbles on underwater surfaces—we knew our process had been rendered obsolete. We hadn't lost to superior sailing, but rather, we had lost to *technology*. A new world of competitive sailing had begun ... and we had caught on too late. The *Stars and Stripes* team, led by Dennis, resolved to never let it happen again.

But how could we change our approach? We already used three highly esteemed naval architects to create our boat designs. How could we improve on that? We weren't technologists; we were businessmen and sailors. We gave ourselves a few months to lick our wounds, take stock on what had happened, and plot our new, technology-driven approach.

Walter Cronkite gives me a briefing in 1984.

Dennis in particular needed that break. He had been the focus of much of the blame. The Cup had resided in glory at the NYYC since 1851, where it had been successfully defended for more than 130 years. Now it was gone. The joke had long been that if and when the NYYC lost the America's Cup, it would be replaced by the head of the losing captain. It wasn't a joke anymore. Dennis was so shattered by the loss that he wouldn't even speak about it until the following January.

Then, in February 1984, I got a call from Science Applications International Corporation (SAIC). It grew to be the largest employee-owned research and engineering company in the United States, but in those days the company was working out of a small building in La Jolla. I remember the drive there with Dennis—and as we pulled up to their building, he said, "Let's not waste more than thirty minutes with these guys."

Once the SAIC team started their presentation, I was ready to cut the meeting to ten minutes—especially after they told us they had never worked on a boat hull before. But the more I listened, the more I realized that if we were ever going to win back the Cup, we would need a radically new approach—and that these guys could give us just such a revolutionary design. Dennis agreed. Three hours later, it took only a handshake to sign a deal with SAIC.

And with that handshake, we committed ourselves to making the biggest wave possible. If the next America's Cup was going to be decided by technology, then we were committing everything to be the technological leader.

I spent years watching Dennis Conner's career grow.
I knew he was the right man to bring home the America's Cup.

SAIC took up the challenge with impressive intensity. Working at a Seattle wind tunnel, the team embarked on a keel redesign every bit as revolutionary as the Australians'. SAIC's was even more far reaching because the resulting upturned wings' design—which shed drag on their tips—would ultimately help to create the upwardly bent wing tips we've all become accustomed to seeing on commercial airliners. The reduced drag that helps a 747 save on fuel in the air was what helped us race faster through the water.

Despite its inexperience in the water, SAIC knew what it was doing in design, and unexpectedly, the real challenge turned out not to be the technology per se but our relationship to it. Frankly, Dennis and I could barely understand what the SAIC engineers were talking about. Luckily, we did know who could: sail maker and main sail "trimmer" John Marshall. By happy coincidence, he talked tech, and so he became our go-between.

Still, it was an unusual relationship. SAIC was *nothing* like what we were used to in the sailing world. It was filled with people in beards and flip-flops working at computers and talking in scientific lingo so obscure that even Marshall sometimes had trouble translating it. But the results we were seeing were stunning. Slowly our old optimism and competitiveness returned. We were going to be ready for the Australians.

The new SAIC designs also brought back Dennis's confidence. When he was ready, I approached him about going back to the NYYC as a way of showing our commitment to restoring the Cup to its rightful home. When he agreed, we approached the NYYC with just that proposal. Their reply was, "Let us get back to you in two weeks."

So we waited. We knew the NYYC was entertaining several other similar applications, but we assumed that they were coming to a decision. The two weeks passed—then another two weeks. We called periodically, only to be told that the decision was still being made. Finally we were told that the Club was considering a competition for sponsorship among several other applicants. More calls. Eventually, we gave up; it was becoming obvious that, after our defeat, the NYYC wasn't anxious for us to come back on its team.

But we were undaunted. It was time to make some more waves. We decided to sponsor ourselves. We agreed that Dennis would head the Cup team, and I would run the syndicate sponsoring the team.

We didn't make an auspicious start: the press conference at which we announced our decision to mount a separate assault on the America's Cup on behalf of the San Diego Yacht Club drew a total of *six* people.

But even that didn't slow us down. We knew that we had a great troika team in Dennis, SAIC, and me. SAIC came up with a brilliant and revolutionary new design, I found the sponsorship to build the stable of three boats, and in the waters off Hawaii, Dennis trained an unmatched team to the peak of performance. In 1987, four years after our loss, we were ready to meet the Australians again, this time in their home waters of Fremantle, Western Australia.

There were a total of ten challengers from around the world, each anxious to become the final entry to battle the Aussies and become the America's Cup champions. It took some thirty-five elimination races over three and one-half months for our boat, *Stars and Stripes*, to prevail. Now we were ready for the Aussies.

I vividly remember that first race. As we were towed out, tens of thousands of people lined the harbor breakwater, 90 percent of them waving the Australian flag. But we weren't intimidated; we knew that we had the best boat and crew. And we had specifically trained off Hawaii because it duplicated conditions caused by the *Fremantle Doctor*—the local name of a healthy, consistent fifteen- to twenty-five-knot wind that makes for choppy water but great sailing. We were as ready to compete as we would ever be.

It goes without saying that I wished I could have been crewing aboard *Stars and Stripes* as it raced. But it wasn't to be, so I did the next best thing. Under the rules, we were allowed one twenty-foot support boat tracking our race boat at no closer than one hundred yards. So I went out every day on that second boat, and at the end of each race, I'd hop aboard the race boat for the ride back, debriefing the crew on everything I'd seen from my unique perspective.

Roberta and I are all smiles after the last America's Cup race in 1987.

Looking back, the experience was a high point of my life. I was fifty-six years old and chairman of the *Stars and Stripes* syndicate. And if Dennis was captain on the water, I was the person who had raised the money, built the three boats, and managed the logistics of getting boats and crews back and forth between locations across half of the world.

We won that first race. As we were being towed out the next day, I noticed that there were a few more American flags waving in the crowd along the breakwater. And when we won that second race, there were even more American flags. Australians, it seems, love to win. But they also love a winner. And in 1987 we weren't only winners; we were their champions as well.

In the end, we won in four straight races. And on that last championship morning, a majority of the flags being waved were for the *Stars and Stripes*.

The days that followed were a blur. As I write this, I'm looking at a painting on the wall of my office of our boat cutting through the rough water at Fremantle as it rounds a mark. It was tough sailing, but we had triumphed.

The award ceremony was the next day at the Perth Yacht Club in front of hundreds of cheering sailing fans. I have in my home a photograph of that day. Our team sat at a table on a raised dais. At one end of the same table stood the America's Cup itself. My photograph captures the end of the ceremony, when audience members came up to congratulate us and old friends came to say hello. In the photo I'm talking to some of those friends … casually leaning my elbow on the Cup as if I never had any doubt that it would be ours.

*Here I stand with the America's Cup at the awards ceremony
following the 1987 races in Perth, Australia.*

*Roberta and I hosted Governor Ronald Reagan before he began
his eight years as our fortieth president.*

Now it was time to fly home. Indeed, within minutes of
stepping on land after the final race, I had gone back to my
duties, including phoning Continental Airlines to charter our
flight home.

We landed first in Hawaii to refuel and used the time to
thank our support team for the three summers we had spent
training there. Then it was on to San Diego, where the mayor
met us and a motorcade took us to city hall for a celebration
among fellow citizens of our home city. Then we were on another
plane, this time to Washington, DC, to be honored by President
Reagan and Vice President Bush. I was hugely honored that they
had invited the eleven members of the race team and me for a
reception in the Oval Office of the White House.

The next day we went to New York for a welcoming parade up
Fifth Avenue. In addition to Dennis and me, on our float were the

mayors of San Diego and New York. That night we had dinner with our wives and Donald Trump at his favorite Manhattan restaurant, Le Cirque.

But sailing competition, the America's Cup most of all, never really ends. There is no final winner—just the next race. It came sooner than we ever expected.

San Diego was supposed to announce the site for the next Cup defense but had assumed that there was no hurry. Thus, by the rules, we had to accept any challenge. That's when a rogue challenge arrived from New Zealand—for ten months hence—and caught us unprepared.

Worse, the Kiwis had already been working for six weeks on a wholly new craft—120 feet long, or more than three times as long as the twelve-meter boats the United States, the Australians, and other competitors had used for a generation. The New Zealand boat violated the spirit of the competition, but it was just under the size limit decreed by the Cup's original deed.

Named head of the San Diego Defense Committee, I realized two things: (1) that we had to move very fast if we weren't going to default, and (2) that the age of the traditional America's Cup competition was over.

The die was now cast. It was time to throw away the old design book and come up with a solution we could execute not in years but in months. In the end, we decided to make waves again: we would compete with a sixty-foot, dual-hulled catamaran. Needless to say, that news, once it leaked out, opened a few eyes around the competitive sailing community, since a catamaran had never before competed in the America's Cup.

Finally, the date of our first race had arrived, and we were barely ready. As we had proposed and hoped, our "David," a sixty-foot catamaran, easily beat their "Goliath" in four straight races.

• • •

Then, if you remember the news stories that were carried around the world, the Kiwi syndicate sued us. They had been so convinced of their impending triumph—only to see it dashed—that they decided to take the fight off the water, onto dry land, and into the courts. They thought they'd been very clever with their new boat design, but they had been "out-clevered" by us. They claimed we had an illegal boat. We knew better.

The Kiwis won the first court case in New York, where the original Cup Deed of Gift was recorded. But we won the second round on appeal, and most importantly, we won the third and decisive trial. We won and kept the America's Cup.

In the span of just five years, we had lost and then twice won the America's Cup on the water as well as lost and won it again in the courts. One can't ask for much more excitement in the sailing world in such a compressed period of time. I was weary but happy.

In the end I stayed on, leading the San Diego committee through one more Cup defense four years later. In one respect, the 1992 race was a welcome return to tradition: the two boats, *America* and Italy's *Il Moro di Venezia V* were identical. For me, on the other hand, everything had changed: it was a different crew, a different syndicate, and most of all, a different captain. Dennis Conner, his reputation more than restored, had retired from America's Cup racing.

We won in four races. It seemed a perfect time to retire, and I did so soon after the victory celebration. Capping our careers, Dennis and I were elected to the America's Cup Hall of Fame at the Herreshoff Marine Museum in Bristol, Rhode Island.

Many friends were made during my America's Cup period—friendships that continue to this day. I also have many mementos and honors from that time. Of all of those items, the one I return to most—because it still teaches me—is a framed, etched-glass memento given to me by President Reagan that day in the White House, inscribed with these words:

To Malin Burnham:

There is no limit to what
man can do or where he can go,
if he doesn't mind who gets the credit.

With best wishes,
Ronald Reagan

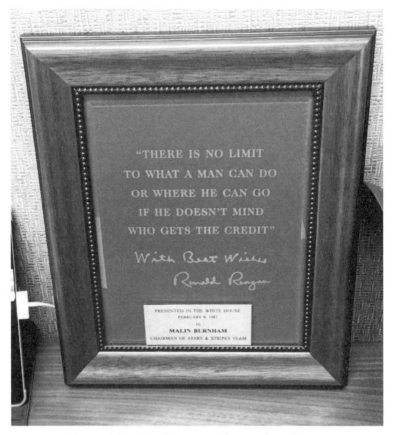

"THERE IS NO LIMIT
TO WHAT A MAN CAN DO
OR WHERE HE CAN GO
IF HE DOESN'T MIND
WHO GETS THE CREDIT"

With Best Wishes

Ronald Reagan

PRESENTED IN THE WHITE HOUSE
FEBRUARY 9, 1987
TO
MALIN BURNHAM
CHAIRMAN OF STARS & STRIPES TEAM

My award from President Reagan for my role as chairman
of the winning America's Cup team in 1987.

I was sixty-two years old. My America's Cup career was now behind me. It was time to go out and make some new waves.

A postscript: When I won the world championship in 1945, I was the youngest sailing champion in the world. Now, because I won at such a young age and have lived so long, I have been the longest-standing sailing world champion, perhaps of all time.

As I wrote this book, I achieved another milestone. With me as skipper, our team won the thirty-fifth running of the International Masters Regatta—two weeks before my eighty-eighth birthday. As one of my crew members suggested, I now have the second bookend on my sailing career. In addition to being the youngest ever to win the International Star Class World Championship at age seventeen, I am now, seventy years later, the oldest to have won the Masters.

I've been told this makes me both the youngest and oldest sailing world champion ever, as well as the individual with the longest interval between championships. It's a wonderful way to finish what I began so long ago.

Proud sponsors of our America's Cup team.

CHAPTER 4

KNOW THYSELF
(AND THY COMMITMENTS)

I've spent the second half of my life engaged in philanthropy, and one of the most important things I've learned is that when it comes to serving your community, you will change. So will your community. For that reason, from time to time, I find it very useful to take inventory of my various community obligations.

While relaxing at our vacation home in Los Cabos, Mexico, a few years ago, I sat down with a yellow pad and started writing all my commitments to boards, committees, and projects. It took me four days to remember all of them.

The list totaled thirty-five different organizations, for which I chaired or cochaired fourteen. Frankly, I was shocked. I knew I was heavily committed, but I had no idea I was *that* committed. Looking at the list, I wondered how I managed to do it all.

The truth was, I realized, that I couldn't do it all. No one human being can do justice to that kind of load. I realized that

I wasn't being fair to all those organizations that depended on me to give them my best.

The moment I saw that list, I realized that my current situation was untenable and that many of my current commitments could be better served by someone else with the time and the focus. So I began to prioritize. Those organizations where I could be most helpful by staying on board remained on my list. For those organizations where I could be most helpful by retiring and letting someone more valuable take my place, I did just that—leaving a cushion of time, of course, for those entities to find my replacement.

The effect was noticed almost immediately. Both groups were better off, and those where I stayed hopefully benefitted because I then had the time and interest to be more useful and productive than ever.

It was in the early 1980s that Roberta and I decided it was time for us to formalize our philanthropic donations. From the very beginning of my career, we had always given money to charity. For years, Roberta and I would occasionally ask ourselves, "Are we really doing the right thing? Are we making progress? Are we making an impact?"

All we really knew was that we were writing thirty to forty checks per year to various foundations in the San Diego region. Yet we couldn't prove that we were making any real difference to any of them. These checks were relatively small dollar amounts. Small dollars usually mean a weak voice, and without a strong voice, you really don't have much influence over the fate of your money. As I had done with my board commitments, we decided to narrow the target of our giving to three or fewer areas of interest.

We had two distinct concerns:

- *Stability.* We would set aside a sufficiently large amount of capital so that our philanthropic efforts would not be cyclical, unpredictable, or in need of constant replenishment.
- *Frequency.* We would give consistent amounts of financial support to our target recipients in both strong and weak economies.

The good news was that even as we were pondering how to proceed with this reconfiguration of our giving, one of our security investments was making our decision much easier: it was now worth ten times our original investment.

We had several options. After conversing with some of my business mentors together with our tax advisors, Roberta and I decided to form our own private foundation. We obtained the IRS approval for a 501(c)(3) foundation and contributed that hugely successful windfall stock in its entirety to our new personal foundation.

Now we needed to develop a giving plan. Since we didn't have any outstanding philanthropic commitments, we decided to take plenty of time to plan a long-term program. This turned out to be a fortuitous decision because the stock we had contributed to the foundation continued to increase in value over several more years. Our stock success gave the foundation a very strong financial footing. It also gave us another good reason for long-term planning.

Taking our time as we determined our targets proved to be one of the smartest things we ever did. In addition to increasing our stock windfall, we were able to challenge many of our preconceptions and discovered that many of our priorities and interests had changed over the years. Many of the areas that had captured our attention a quarter century before had either changed dramatically during that time or had simply lost their attraction to Roberta and me. Meanwhile, two fields that had barely entered our consciousness when we were younger now seemed to call out for our attention and needed our help. Those two fields were health and education.

Some people we knew were surprised by our choices, especially regarding education. After all, I was the first member of my family to go to college, and I didn't study health or medicine. What they didn't appreciate was the difference between *experience* and *interest*. We may not have had extensive resumes in these fields, but we had a deep and abiding interest—and had done extensive reading—in both of them. We may not have been experts, at least at the beginning, but we knew enough to appreciate where we could help.

Now that we had determined our two primary fields of interest, Roberta and I could deepen our research and investigations into those fields. Ultimately, after a great deal of thoughtful examination, we developed a strategic plan. This plan further refined our giving. We would support education from kindergarten to grad school, and we would give to health research.

That plan was the crucial component that had been missing from our philanthropy up to that point. I recommend the creation of such a plan to everyone entering into the world of giving. In retrospect, having a strategy enabled us to make smart and—just as important—*disciplined* choices.

Without question, we made the correct decision in narrowing our giving and sticking to a plan, because from that time and right up to the present, it's clear that our gifts have actually advanced our causes. The impact of our giving, scattered and shallow before, is now both focused and deep.

After a few years using this plan and refining both our giving and our commitments, we looked back and were pleased with the results. We found that we were more involved with our targeted charities, communicated with them a lot more, and were receiving not just thank-you notes but actual requests for our opinions. We could see at last that we were making a difference.

Crucial to these new relationships with nonprofits (and contrary to the philosophy of many philanthropists) was that we didn't demand any board positions to protect our contributions. That's not to say that we weren't asked, and sometimes we accepted board seats. But we didn't ask for them. We let the charities decide if we were needed.

This approach reflects a larger belief of mine: never try to tell someone what to do, and that includes my family, my friends, and my business associates. We pass around ideas and talk about things, but I never try to force my views on others. Needless to say, this is not common practice among most men and women in my position. On the contrary, for many people, the reward for being successful is precisely the fact that you get to tell other people what to do. All I can say is that my philosophy has worked out very well for me. I have a better relationship with others and enjoy more respect. Most important, I achieve better and more enduring results. And isn't that the point of telling people what to do?

I'm often asked whether I'm giving up too much control over the fate of our money by not demanding a board seat on the nonprofits into which we put that money. Why, others ask, do I give up my chance at governance? How do I make sure our money is being used well?

There are two answers to that.

First, taking a board seat often means that you have *less* rather than more control over your giving. Let me explain. Typically, in taking a board seat, you have either given money to the organization in the recent past or are expected to do so in the near future. In other words, you are expected to adjust your giving to the organization's schedule. That pulls you off your strategic plan. I'm not willing to do that. We want to give on our own schedule.

Second, we can govern our own philanthropy by giving not to the organization itself but to a particular project we deem worthy and congruent to our plan *within* that organization. Thus, if we want to give to the YMCA, our check would go not to the national office of that distinguished organization but rather to a new facility or program that we have determined has a need for that funding.

We also back up that contribution and track its effectiveness by expecting regular reports on the results of our giving. We make it a point to stipulate up front that we expect, at the very least, an annual report for the first three to five years on the construction of the facility or the implementation of the program and how it is proceeding toward its avowed goals.

When we read these reports, we look for three things:
- Is there an actual need for this new project or facility?
- Is it well designed?
- Is it well managed?

If we don't see acceptable answers to any one of those three questions in the annual report, then it's time to intervene. Without the right answers, then it is likely that we will end our commitment. It is precisely because we warn the recipients of our expectations from the start that Roberta and I are rarely disappointed.

To see how all this works, let's take a closer look at two of our largest philanthropic projects.

The Malin Burnham Center for Civic Engagement is part of the San Diego Foundation (SDF), a community foundation started forty years ago that currently manages $760 million in total assets. The SDF has given away more than $850 million over its organizational lifetime. It is one of the city's greatest assets, and I'm proud to have been affiliated with the SDF for its entire history.

Twenty years ago, the SDF was half the size it is today. I was working with the new CEO in an advisory role and on and off as a board member.

Now, community foundations typically do not want to get involved in politics; it can divide members and increases the odds of getting dragged into a controversy that can damage the organization's image or force everyone to choose sides. On the other hand, community foundations gain more expertise about certain slices of local society than any other kind of organization. Homelessness and forest-fire prevention are two examples: the SDF became the target of giving for people displaced by local fires. This hard-earned expertise can be hugely valuable to policy makers—if foundations are willing to share it.

It was my belief that on these specialty matters, the SDF should stand up and be heard. It was not a popular position to take. The CEO and many of the board members of the SDF understood the value of this expertise—but they also worried about the dangers of taking a public position on its use. I bided my time and waited for the right moment.

That moment came when Dr. Richard Florida (then of Carnegie Mellon, now of the University of Toronto) was invited to San Diego to talk about his new book on innovation centers around the world. At the end of his talk, Dr. Florida joined a dozen of us for a private meeting. It was at this meeting that someone asked, "What do we do with someone who has a new idea for our community?"

Dr. Florida's answer surprised us. He suggested that we create a new institute specifically chartered to accept and investigate ideas for new programs submitted by anyone in our community.

It appeared to be a good concept, but I otherwise dismissed the idea for a reason that was based on my own experience: new entities have no clout. They lack profile, footprint, and networks. However, other people seemed to agree with Dr. Florida, because the next time I heard this idea, it was being presented by the SDF as one of its own operations, to be called the Center for Civic Engagement.

This announcement completely changed my mind. Having the SDF behind it would give the Center precisely the muscle and presence it would need to succeed and have a real impact from the start. When the SDF asked me to endow the Center, I was happy to sign on. I've been the major supporter of the Center for Civic Engagement for three years now, and I'm very proud of the result.

The Center serves as a kind of funnel. New ideas arrive from anyone in the San Diego community, without prejudice, at the big end of the funnel. The center's team researches the viability and potential effectiveness of the idea. When and if everything works, out of the small end of the funnel comes a realistic, fundable project.

As chartered, the Center only serves as the architect of ideas, not the contractor; anyone who wants to shepherd the idea to its real-life execution must find some other entity in the San Diego community to fund and manage it. This removes the Center from the politics and the complex, time-consuming process of fundraising and instead lets it focus on what it does best.

These days, I don't have day-to-day involvement in either the SDF or the Center for Civic Engagement. At its founding forty years ago, I was deeply involved with the SDF as a trustee—but it is a measure of its success over the last four decades that I no longer feel the need to be that engaged.

Sometimes I try to play the role of Bernard Baruch, the famous advisor to US presidents a century ago. Baruch held his conversations with the powerful on a park bench. Board members are regularly looking for new ideas, and I'm happy to comply. At the same time, I'm updated on the Center's status two or three times per year. I love both the SDF and the Center, but I measure their success by how much they *don't* need me to be there all of the time. My ego doesn't require me to be irreplaceable.

Burnham-Moores Center for Real Estate partners, John Moores, and me holding an award from the Woodrow Wilson International Center for Scholars, an organization that fosters scholarship and dialogue in the humanities and social sciences.

The Burnham-Moores Center for Real Estate (CRE) is a real estate school within the business school at the University of San Diego (USD). John Moores, who partnered with me in the major underwriting of the CRE, is an entrepreneur who made his fortune in the Internet world. He moved from Texas to San Diego about twenty-five years ago and moved back three years ago. During his San Diego years, John was best known as the owner of the San Diego Padres and as the man responsible for building the city's downtown baseball stadium, Petco Park. He was also a partner of mine in several real estate projects.

As an owner and partner, I love watching the Padres play.

Why the CRE? Because San Diego is one of the most dynamic real estate markets in the country. It deserved to have a top-notch real estate school to train real estate professionals to work here. Just as important, several of us believed that the city should have just such a program and were in the position to make it happen.

But how would we do it? How would we create a new school that would have a major presence and impact from the start, without years or decades of ramp-up? Once again, I went back to my principle that it is better to piggyback on an existing institution than to start from scratch. Happily, John agreed with me that we should build our thought center at an established business school. We settled on USD rather than the giant UCSD or San Diego State University (SDSU) because USD was a growing institution, it was an independent, private university, and it already had a highly rated business school.

The good news was that the leadership of USD loved the idea. We agreed that the first step was for a small group of us philanthropists to put up $1.5 million to endow a chair in hopes of attracting a top director to the still nonexistent CRE. Once in place, he or she would both legitimize the program and attract other faculty talent. Once we successfully recruited that director, we went on to endow even more professorial chairs. Our total endowment was $5 million—a bargain for what was accomplished.

That was twenty-two years ago. A dozen years ago, USD was gracious enough to put John's and our family names on the CRE. We were all deeply honored.

• • •

It has now been thirty-four years since Roberta and I started our foundation and fourteen years since we belatedly developed our strategic plan for the foundation. My only regret is that we didn't start with both sooner.

Here are some of the lessons we've learned over those years that you may find useful:

1. *Start early.* If you have been in any way successful, consider beginning the process of giving back earlier rather than later.

2. *Don't do stand-alone programs.* They take too long to build, they start with zero credibility, and they have no profile and few connections. Instead, bolt your new institution to a more established one.

3. *Choose deep and wide fields for your charitable commitments.* Follow what interests you but not so narrowly that you needlessly reduce your options.

4. *You will change.* What interests you at age fifty may no longer do so when you are seventy. Don't stick with what you no longer care about; be willing to move your contributions.

5. *Focus on making a difference.* Awards and titles are nice, but the older you get, the more you'll find that what really matters is that you've made a difference— that your contributions have been meaningful.

6. *Keep your giving targeted.* Try not to give to foundations' general funds. Rather, only give to independent institutions for specific uses.

7. *Demand regular audits.* As part of your initial commitment, require regular updates on the impact of your giving and the progress of the recipient.

8. *Live long.* The flip side of starting early is to live a long time. One reason is that time enables you to develop an expertise in and deep understanding of the targets of your giving and your strategic plan. A second reason is that you can see the real effect of your efforts. And the third reason is that you will inevitably run into roadblocks—usually put up by bureaucrats—to your philanthropic efforts. Sometimes the only solution is to simply "outlive the bastards." The only way to do that is stick with what you believe until you win, even if it takes decades.

9. *Stay Alive.* The corollary to number eight is that it is not enough to live a long time; you need to stay healthy in order to perform your tasks. Some of the principle influencers on a person's physical health are habit and discipline. In my case, I was fortunate to start early. Upon graduating from college, I weighed 183 pounds, and I committed to stay within the range of 183 and 185 pounds—where I remain to this day. How? It's really quite easy. Every morning, just before I enter my shower, I step on the bathroom scale. I refer to this procedure as my "dessert determinator."

I've found another easy way to trick my brain. At lunch and dinner, I seldom entirely clean my plate. This reminds me that I am full. Moreover, once one's plate has been cleaned of food, it's easy to go back for seconds.

Of course, it's also helpful to have a regular stretching and exercise routine. Every morning, starting before getting out of bed, I begin my stretching regime, followed by more strenuous activities on the floor. One other great activity, especially for us older folks, is to practice standing on one leg at a time for several seconds. This gives us much better ability to recover before falling when tripping upon a raised sidewalk or unfamiliar stairs. And then there are many sports in which we can participate into our senior years. My favorites have been sailing, handball, snow skiing, and golf.

10. *Think legacy.* Nobody lives forever. What happens to your foundation and other family assets after you are gone? Many philanthropists, now dead, would be heartbroken to see where their money is going. Talk to a tax expert now about your legacy—don't wait until it is too late.

11. *Stay engaged.* Delegate duties when you can, and always measure the success of your philanthropic efforts by how little they need you over time. But use that independence and time to search out new ways to contribute. Keep up your schedule—if you rest, you rust.

CHAPTER 5

PURPOSEFUL GIVING

Simple giving isn't enough; it also has to be smart and strategic. Most of all, giving has to be *purposeful.* Needless to say, many recipients want philanthropy without strings, but if you want to have any control over the effect of your largesse, you need those strings. The trick is to keep the strings few and precisely connected to the project.

Wherever we can, Roberta and I try to make our giving purposeful to add ideas, direction, and long-term planning to our money. We are not the kind of people who write checks, walk away, and hope that everything works out well. We want to help control the fate of our good works.

One form of purposeful giving that has given us much personal pleasure is *scholarships.* Let me tell you the remarkable story of two of those scholarships.

Each spring in San Diego, the internationally acclaimed Kyoto Prize organization holds a three-day celebration of its three current laureates, each an important global figure. One feature of this event is the awarding of six one-year college scholarships to high school seniors, half from each side of the San Diego/Tijuana border.

I had initiated—and at the time chaired—the Kyoto Prize Symposium for our area. We put in place a team of five researchers to vet all scholarship candidates. They loved the work. Rodrigo Ortega from Tijuana was one of the three young high school students to whom we awarded the 2006 scholarship. Rodrigo's life had been tough. His father, a medical doctor, had been killed in an automobile accident when the boy was two. A few years later, his mother was kidnapped and ended up paying all the family's assets in a ransom to free herself. With her career as an artist and photographer bringing in little income, Rodrigo's mom decided to move with her son from Mexico City to Tijuana. There, despite the challenge of poverty and life in the public schools, Rodrigo showed himself to be a brilliant student and a worthy recipient of a Kyoto scholarship.

Rodrigo Ortega overcame so many hardships to become a strong student and a worthy Kyoto scholarship award-winner.

Following the ceremony for that award, Rodrigo and his mother sought us out to thank us. After just ten minutes of conversation with the young man, Roberta and I looked at each other and agreed, "This kid is going places." You could just feel it and see it: his eye contact, his attention, his handshake—the little things that say that you are speaking to a powerful personality and intellect.

This was in spring 2006, when we held our annual event. In about July of that year, Rodrigo sent us an e-mail excitedly telling us that he had been accepted to the University of Alberta—and would use his scholarship there. It was a bit of a surprise: not many Mexican kids choose to go to college in Canada. But we cheered his decision.

There was a second reason for the e-mail. Might it be possible, Rodrigo asked, for us to help him one more time? The scholarship, he said, would get him to the University of Alberta, and his mom would help with transportation and books. But he still needed help with housing. Might we help him find a place to live?

It was a sizable request but not an unreasonable one. We weren't willing to just write a check; part of purposeful giving is that you maintain close contact with recipients so that you can more precisely gauge both their commitment and their actual need.

We met with Rodrigo and his mom. There was much to talk about, but first we had an obvious question: Why Alberta? Rodrigo had the perfect answer: among all of the universities in North America, Alberta offered the specialized degree he wanted to pursue—a combination of science and medicine. His answer was well thought out and reasonable.

So our foundation set up an account for Rodrigo at a local credit union in San Diego, and he and his mother set off for Canada. Not only did we underwrite his first year's housing expense, but we have also been covering all of his education and housing costs ever since.

Rodrigo finished his degree four years later. Not surprisingly, he graduated with honors. He came back to San Diego during two of those summers and interned at the Burnham Institute. He worked with a number of scientists during these internships, and all came back with glowing reports of his intelligence, professionalism, and work ethic.

Following graduation, Rodrigo decided that he wanted to spend two more years in Canada doing graduate work. The professor who served as his mentor at the University of Alberta had moved her research to the University of Lethbridge, and Rodrigo wanted to follow her there. Our foundation supported him in that endeavor as well. As I write this, he has just received his master's degree from Lethbridge. He's now deciding whether to go to medical school or earn a PhD and pursue a career in research.

Whatever Rodrigo decides, I hope he also decides to return and work in the San Diego/Tijuana area. Of course, that isn't necessary—he will leave his mark wherever he goes. Still, we have all but adopted Rodrigo and his mother as part of our family, and we would like him to work right here. Either way, we believe he will enjoy a very successful career.

This is the essence of purposeful giving: it is directed, intimate, and adaptable. When you become that close to your recipients, you don't force them into a predetermined path; you adapt to the changes that happen in their lives. Best of all, you get to enjoy their success *with* them, not just read about it in an annual report.

Another act of purposeful giving in the form of a personal scholarship involved my late secretary and personal assistant, Sue Russell.

Sue was a wonderful person. She worked for my company for more than twenty years—the last six exclusively with me—before she died suddenly and unexpectedly of a stomach hemorrhage. We were all shocked and heartbroken at her death; having worked with Sue so closely, I felt her loss especially deeply. I resolved to do something in her memory.

Sue had never attended college before she joined Burnham Real Estate Company. Being a person with lots of foresight and ambition, she enrolled at SDSU in nighttime classes. It took her twelve years to graduate, but she persevered.

So when the shock of her passing finally wore off, we decided to endow a scholarship in Sue's name at SDSU. We limited potential recipients to students pursuing women's studies majors with a minor in political science, English, or business administration. Why? Because this track duplicates Sue's college experience—so with luck, more Sue Russells will be created by this scholarship. Of course, Sue herself can never be duplicated, but now she has a permanent memorial. The program is currently in its third year.

Another of our scholarship funds was established within my alma mater, the engineering department at Stanford University. One condition we set for Stanford was that preference be given to a San Diego resident, if one was available, because I want to see more San Diegans enjoy the education experience that I enjoyed.

About four years ago, I was approached by the commodore of the San Diego Yacht Club with a request. It was to help pay for half of the cost of a new building. This project taught me about a new kind of purposeful giving.

Some background: The San Diego Yacht Club leases its site on San Diego Bay from our port district. Every thirty or forty years, when the port's land leases come up for extensions, each tenant is required to bring its structures up to current standards. In our case, the yacht club had designed a new ten-thousand-square-foot, two-story building to house our junior sailing program. The design included classrooms with the latest instructional video screens, a full-workout gym, offices for coaches and member volunteers, and repair bays for the club's fleet of sailboats.

It would be an important contribution to the community: the San Diego Yacht Club offers its junior sailing program to 250 kids each summer, 20 to 30 percent of them children of nonmembers. The new facilities would also serve as the home venue for the sailboat racing programs of a half-dozen high schools in the area.

Typically in the past, when the San Diego Yacht Club decided to make improvements on its facilities—usually a matter of a few hundred thousand dollars—it simply assessed its 1,600 members for the amount. Now, for the first time, the club's leadership had decided to try something new and approach individual members.

There are two more things you need to know. First, commodores are in office for just one year, so whatever initiatives they start, they have to complete in a hurry. Second, the yacht club prints out an annual roster that tracks membership longevity, so when a member dies who has longer tenure than you, you move up one place in the list. I had been poised at number two in longevity for a long time—and happily so. Roberta said, "Never get to number one—there's no future there." As it happens, a few months before I wrote this book, I became number one—and though I get a little more respect, I guess, I'm still not happy about it.

Needless to say, being number two put me at the top of a lot of lists—including funding sources for the new building construction. The proposal made by the commodore of the club, with the vice commodore sitting beside him, was that I would underwrite half of the cost of that construction ($3 million total), and the new facility would be named the Malin Burnham Sailing Center. "You're the first person we're approaching," they told me. Yeah, I'd heard that one before.

All through that ninety-minute breakfast, I kept silently asking myself, "Why me?" I knew there were many other club members who might want this opportunity. I told the commodore that I would get back to him within two weeks.

I spent a few days recalling the life-changing experiences I had enjoyed in the San Diego Yacht Club junior sailing program as a teenager seventy years before. I realized that giving the under-writing was the right thing to do, both for the yacht club and as a way to honor my own past. I also knew that I wasn't just going to write a check—as always, I was going to exercise the right to guide my contribution.

Two weeks later, to start our next meeting, I told the commodore that I would agree to his gift request—he was thrilled—on one condition. I slid in front of him a sheet of paper containing the following words:

Virtues of Excellence

Plan Ahead—Set personal goals.

Commitment—Take responsibility.

Hard Work—Be prepared.

Dedication—Never give up.

Teamwork—Everyone contributes.

Play by the Rules—Be honest, ethical, and fair.

Follow Through—Take action to achieve your goals.

It was a distillation of everything I had learned in my life and career. The San Diego Yacht Club, though it didn't know it, had forced me to sit down and take stock of myself, to ask myself: What acquired wisdom would I convey to my own fifteen-year-old, junior sailor self after seven decades of victories, losses, failures, and successes? How would I convey this wisdom to a new generation of young sailors on the threshold of adulthood?

Once I had written down those principles, I realized that I didn't just want to have them handed out to young people to be glanced at and tossed aside. Rather, I wanted them taught continuously to our future junior sailing classes. I wanted the principles to be omnipresent as a perpetual reminder for the junior sailors to do their best with the highest levels of integrity. I wanted the yacht club's junior sailing program to be more than just competitive; I wanted it to teach young people much more than just how to steer a sailboat.

So when that moment came to stipulate the demands attached to my underwriting, I pointed to the sheet of paper I'd put in front of the commodore and told him that I wanted those words permanently attached to the new building—and in more than one location. I told him I didn't want to come back in five years and discover that the precepts had been forgotten.

Ultimately the commodore, the board of directors, and the junior sailing supporters of the San Diego Yacht Club all agreed. And today, you can see that list of virtues in big letters, affixed to three different places on the new center.

As I said at the beginning of this chapter, Roberta and I want our giving to always be more than writing a check. To be purposeful means to be both focused and personal. It means attaching the right strings: not for our own benefit but as a way to benefit the community. It means keeping ourselves involved mentally even when, given the press of other commitments, we can no longer be involved physically. The challenge is to devise those strings so that the recipient sees them as an asset rather than a burden.

Purposeful giving also doesn't end with the giving. I've told you the story of Rodrigo Ortega and his mother: a scholarship award that has bloomed into a personal friendship. The same outcome has proven true, in a slightly different way, with the Stanford scholars. At least three-quarters of those scholarship recipients have contacted me, sometimes years after graduation. Many are at a fork in the road professionally and want some advice about how to proceed. Others just want to say hello. Roberta and I cherish all of those relationships.

A final thought: implicit in the word *purposeful* is the notion of *directedness.* I think that is both accurate and misleading. When we give purposefully, we "direct" our philanthropy toward specific goals, specific institutions, and specific individuals. We also want to maintain some "direction" over the application of those funds so that they are used wisely and fulfill our specific goals. That said, the one thing we don't want our purposeful giving to do is "direct" the recipients in such a way that we narrow their options or limit their opportunities. The strings we attach are not there to restrain them but rather to help them climb even higher.

CHAPTER 6

CHARITIES ARE BUSINESSES TOO!

Too often, charities—because they appeal to our emotions—are thought to be exempt from the normal rules of business, from management to accounting to productivity.

This is a terrible mistake. Successful charities—that is, those that have the maximum impact and achieve their goals—are *always* well-run businesses as well. Having a good heart is not enough. All charities are good hearted, want to do the right thing, and have the interests of their recipients at heart. Despite this, many charities fade away, and many survive but do a mediocre job. Those that do their job well and thrive over time are those that understand that a charity is also a business—albeit without the need to make a profit for its investors and shareholders.

Sometimes the best thing you can bring to a charity is *discipline*—holding it to the rules of business, including rigorous financial management, even if it means tearing the enterprise down and starting over or walking away.

One of my most challenging board assignments came early in my career, in 1965, when the San Diego City Council decided to purchase and operate what was then a private municipal bus system.

The San Diego Transit Corporation (SDTC) was formed from five veteran business leaders, including me. We were charged with negotiating the purchase price, financing it, and operating the system. In other words, we were handed an empty vessel and told to make something workable out of it.

Fortunately, all of us directors were active business executives who were familiar with these types of transactions. The one area where we were lacking was actually running a bus system. But with some careful planning, the board divided up into equal organizational responsibilities—and within eighteen months, we had a smoothly running municipal bus system. Just five years later, I felt comfortable enough with the success of the operation that I retired. Subsequently, the SDTC was converted into the San Diego Metropolitan Transit District, which also built and now operates San Diego's well-run trolley system.

The lesson from this experience at the very start of my work with charities and nonprofits is that good, basic business skills are applicable to almost every organization. And those skills, combined with careful planning, a well thought-out strategy, and continuous innovation can overcome almost any lack of experience. We set out to succeed, learned what we needed along the way, maintained our business discipline … and succeeded in the end.

• • •

Another example is the YMCA of San Diego. In the mid-1970s, its executive leadership was growing old and ineffective, and the organization was drifting. It had a longtime CEO who was aging and preparing for retirement. Moreover, the organization, which oversees all sixteen branches of the "Y" in the San Diego area, also was in serious financial straits.

The board created a retirement plan for the president, and I was one of five members of a search committee to find his replacement. We determined that there was no one in the local organization qualified for promotion to take on the daunting task of running the whole organization, so we resolved to undertake a national search.

Our strategy going into that search was to find and recruit an executive from a smaller YMCA who wanted to step up and lead a larger chapter. After a comprehensive effort, we whittled the list down to just five final candidates, each of whom we invited in for personal interviews.

After a long day of individual sessions we all agreed that Rich Collato—at that time the executive of the Hawthorne YMCA chapter in southwest Los Angeles—stood head and shoulders above the others. I fully agreed and was pleased with that conclusion.

That's when the other four committee members informed me that we couldn't afford him. It seemed that Rich was seeking an annual salary of $75,000, while the others were satisfied with our proposed $50,000 offer.

I decided to take control, even though I was not the committee chair. "Time out," I told them. "Look, we all agree that the San Diego Y has serious financial challenges. Good business principles tell us that this is not the time to hire a lesser CEO in order to stick to the budget. Rather, we need to hire the best possible leader to get us out of this mess. We all agree that the best leader is Rich Collato, and if it takes a higher salary to get him here, then it is incumbent on us to find the money to pay him."

I knew it wasn't properly my place to hijack the meeting at that moment, but I also knew it was my duty to the organization to do so. That's why I joined the board, after all: to make the San Diego chapter of the YMCA a success.

After some serious arm-twisting, they all agreed to hire Rich. In the end, our concerns were misplaced. Soon after Rich came on board, we got a happy surprise when he informed us that his Hawthorne YMCA backer, the Van Kamp Foundation, had agreed to continue underwriting his $75,000 salary at the Hawthorne Y for the next three years at San Diego. We had hired the best candidate for the price of an average one.

And we got the right person for the job. Rich Collato stayed with us for more than thirty years, during which time he undertook a brilliant turnaround of the organization. In fact, he built the San Diego YMCA into the second largest Y in the nation—second only to New York—in terms of membership, facilities, and annual budget. By the time Rich retired, the budget of the San Diego YMCA was more than $100 million—

ten times what it was when we recruited him. And to think that we almost lost him while quibbling over just $25,000.

On the other hand and at the other extreme, it is also possible to apply so many rigid rules of business to a nonprofit that you lose sight of what that charity exists to do.

I was once involved in a nonprofit institution—it will remain nameless—that had prudently gone out and recruited successful executives from the business world to serve as its chief operating officer (COO) and chief financial officer (CFO). On paper, this seemed to be a brilliant choice, as day-to-day management and budget management are the two institutional functions where nonprofits most often lose their way.

And yet as time passed, it was increasingly obvious to me that something was missing at this nonprofit; I just couldn't put my finger on it. Both of these executives were fine individuals, and their resumes underscored that they were top-notch executives. Watching them in action, they seemed to be doing everything right: they organized teams, developed and placed advertising, and hired talented subordinates. On the surface, everything seemed right. And yet…

In the end, a book opened my eyes. One of the most admired business books ever written and a personal favorite of mine is Jim Collins's *Good to Great.* I've revisited it regularly over the decades and have become a serious student of its message about the importance of a corporate culture that promotes dedicated and disciplined leadership. During my studies of that book, I learned that Collins had also written a monograph—essentially an addendum to the book—that dealt with a topic of particular pertinence to my life.

As the story goes, after *Good to Great* came out, Collins was giving a talk when someone in the audience asked him if the same rules he had discovered also applied to the nonprofit world. Collins had no answer, so he took his team and spent the next two years coming up with one.

The result was *Good to Great and the Social Sectors*. It is just thirty-five pages long, but it contains more wisdom than volumes ten times as thick. Ultimately, Collins's message comes down to one key point:

In for-profit organizations, leadership is done via position and power. In not-for-profit organizations, leadership is done via persuasion from any level.

Collins describes this difference in leadership styles as that between "executive" and "legislative" management. In the former, typically found in for-profit companies, leaders gather power and then exert it to move the organization in a strategic direction. In not-for-profit organizations, this is almost impossible; the employees, who have made sacrifices in salary, time, and emotional commitment, simply won't respond to coercion. Instead, leadership has to be constructed from a consensus among the staff, from top to bottom. But consensus is a slow and often messy process. To counter that, Collins says, nonprofits must be *more* disciplined than their commercial counterparts, and this discipline must extend throughout the organization—from employees to planning and from resource allocation to governance.

As I read this monograph, I realized that even though I had not explicitly defined it, this had been my task with charities for decades. I had been the guy who demanded ever-greater operational discipline in every organization for which I had volunteered my time and money. Moreover, I had expected that discipline to be greater than I had known in the commercial business world—not least because in for-profit businesses, the struggle for profitability and the demand by shareholders for accountability exert their own discipline.

By comparison, nonprofits have few empirical metrics for measuring success: membership growth, donations, corporate support, and not many others. Almost everything else is pretty subjective. Are the recipients benefitting? Is this a service to the community? Is media coverage positive?

The fact that there are so few external forces constraining nonprofits puts even greater emphasis on internal discipline. And that is why, for that aforementioned nonprofit, we had hired the COO and CFO from the commercial world. They had applied that discipline in spades. Yet despite this, morale was falling, the organization seemed to be losing momentum, and the leadership increasingly seemed to be making executive decisions that were out of synch with the staff.

So what was the source of my disquiet about these two gentlemen? After all, they had fulfilled Jim Collins's requirement for good leadership in a nonprofit—or had they? I went back to Collins's monograph and saw what I had missed. While the two executives had fulfilled the second requirement for running a charity, they had failed at the first. In this new world, they had not made the leap to legislative leadership.

Instead of managing through "legislative" consensus and persuasion, they had remained the "executive" bosses they had been in their earlier careers. That is, they had managed through position and authority, and they expected their subordinates to follow without much question beyond the details about how those orders should be executed.

Needless to say, this only created resentment—to the point of near-mutiny—from the employees at that institution. They had chosen careers in this sector precisely because it was driven not by profits, metrics, and quarterly results but by good works, social responsibility, and service to others. While the efforts of these two executives looked good on paper, the reality was that morale was suffering. Some of the most dedicated employees were looking elsewhere, aspiring to join other institutions more congruent to their career goals. In the end, we suggested to these two executives that their estimable talents might be better served back in the commercial sector.

As this example suggests, finding the proper balance between traditional business principles and the special needs of nonprofits is a tricky one. The solution, I've come to believe, is to mix experienced businesspeople—with their special skills— in with the traditional employees and volunteers of nonprofits—with their heart and commitment—and then thoroughly train each group to deal with the other.

One of the crucial components in the training of business-people to work in the nonprofit sector is to teach them to be open to nontraditional talent. The employee or volunteer who doesn't look or act at all like the kind of person you'd hire for a corporate position may have a special genius for working with the homeless, the artistic, the disabled, or the elderly. That you should not judge a book by its cover is never truer than when managing people in the nonprofit world.

But it also works the other way. Businesspeople are often instantly written off by people who work in charities because they are perceived as somehow tainted by the pursuit of profit. Their business skills are also discounted, as if they are somehow not applicable to the nonprofit world. As I've tried to show, nothing could be further from the truth.

There is also a xenophobic tendency in community-based organizations that gives precedence to "locals" (and to natives most of all), as if they alone can truly understand the local culture. Thus, newcomers, however great their skills, find themselves shut out or not receiving the credit they deserve.

Often, if I'm talking to an appropriate group, I begin with the standard definition of an *immigrant*: a person born in a foreign country but now living in the United States. In addition, I tell my audience, I believe that there is an equally important second definition: anyone who now lives, works, or plays in San Diego who wasn't born here.

I then ask for a show of hands of all those who were born in San Diego County. Typically, about 5 percent to 10 percent of the audience will raise their hands. That's when I point to the rest of the room and say: "See? It's you immigrants who have largely built this great place called San Diego, not us 5 or

10 percenters! So let's give credit where credit is due, and let's stop distinguishing 'real' San Diegans from newcomers. We all have something to contribute."

• • •

We've just seen what happens when traditional business executives try to impose a commercial culture on a charity. Coincidentally, just the opposite happened with another, much larger nonprofit institution in the same field as the first.

In this case, the institution promoted its top scientist to the role of interim director. It seemed a smart idea. The new director was brilliant and celebrated in his field; he understood the underlying technology as well as anyone on the planet and had done a solid job running his department. Who could be better?

Things seemed to be going just fine right up until the day the new director publicly announced that his institution had just entered into a consortium with one of the state's largest universities. It was the first time either the employees or the board of directors had ever heard of this agreement, much less the negotiations leading up to it. As one might have predicted, it turned out that being the autocrat of the laboratory was insufficient training for running the entire billion-dollar organization.

This is hardly a unique scenario. Especially in medical research and healthcare nonprofits, lead scientists often become presidents or directors, in many cases serving both research and administrative roles. Almost as often, the result is a double loss: the organization loses a top-flight scientist and gains a mediocre CEO. To correct the imbalance, the scientist-CEO then devotes too much time to administrative duties and not enough time in the laboratory, where his or her talents are strongest. It's lose-lose. Yet the scientists rarely argue that they aren't up for both jobs, or even for that of CEO alone. Part of that is pride, but just as often it is self-delusion. They convince themselves that because they are the smartest scientists in the place, they must also be the smartest businesspeople.

That's why it's often my job as member of the board of science-oriented institutions to argue against promoting the chief scientist, no matter how smart he or she is or how much he or she wants the job.

Yet another mistake that nonprofits make—and one more reason why their boards need the presence of veteran commercial business professionals—is that they tend to get locked into the nonprofit paradigm. That is, sometimes the work they do presents the opportunity to create a for-profit subsidiary that could be hugely beneficial for everyone involved. But either they don't see that opportunity or they fear it, and the opportunity is lost.

Take the case of what was (at the time) called the Burnham Institute for Medical Research. Almost from its founding we had occasionally taken a medical discovery with the right potential for commercialization and created a subsidiary around it, not least because our scientists were the most knowledgeable about transforming their particular medical research into valuable medical products.

This was excellent training for what was to come. In 1987, when we had just the right new product, we launched a commercial start-up called Telios Pharmaceuticals. Telios proved quite successful and was ultimately acquired in 1995 by a much larger medical product company. Was it worth the trouble? Absolutely. During the time we owned it, Telios contributed more than $9 million in profits to the institute, and that money went to support important new research. It proved to be a nice, win-win scenario.

What this taught me is that there is no need to build the traditional fences between for-profit and not-for-profit enterprises. In fact, I have learned to embrace the mixing of the two. As long as all the players understand that the two entities will operate under different rules, each can help the other.

Such an open-minded attitude also improves the chances for long-term success. Again, consider the story of Telios. Our scientists came up with a new and potentially profitable drug. Traditionally, the only course would have been to license that drug to a big pharmaceutical corporation and let them take it from there. The long-held attitude says that we are the architects; let the contractor do the work.

But we had a second possible strategy: commercializing the drug ourselves and increasing our potential profits. That's what we did. Instead of selling off our new product, we took it to the FDA for approval. We got that approval, and we built Telios to produce the drug and bring it to market.

The very notion of for-profit/not-for-profit hybrids is controversial in some people's minds. They believe that one enterprise can't do both—that the philosophies behind the two halves are simply incompatible. Some even believe that we *shouldn't* do it for moral reasons, as if the profits earned by the commercial side will somehow sully the charitable side. I happen to believe that if the rules are followed and the two parties are properly trained in how to do their work, there should not be a problem.

In the case of such hybrid organizations, leadership ultimately comes down to the board of directors because there are two CEOs/directors running two different enterprises. That's yet another reason for having commercial businesspeople on that board. You may be able to survive as a nonprofit without experienced businesspeople on your board, but it is highly unlikely that your for-profit subsidiary will. Veteran businesspeople understand marketing, sales, and pricing. Just as important, they also understand proper disclosure and rules of governance. They see the tripwires that nonprofit types sometimes fail to discern until it is too late.

As an aside regarding ownership, the general rule we use in dividing up intellectual property (IP) rights at the creation of the subsidiary is to split the IP, with one-third going to the individual scientists, one-third to the mother institution (in this case the institute), and one-third to the business subsidiary. This usually seems fair to everyone and enables us to get underway quickly without a lot of squabbling over ownership.

We also prefer to create a second board of directors for the subsidiary but allow for a lot of overlap in membership.

How does Big Pharma feel about this new model, especially when it creates new potential competitors? Well, in my experience, they've wisely decided that rather than fight us, it's best to join us. In recent years, I've seen a growing interest from the giant companies, who used to only write checks, in actually participating in joint ventures with research institutions.

$$\bullet\ \bullet\ \bullet$$

As you can see, I am a great believer in bringing real-world business experience to the board of any nonprofit institution, be it a simple charity or a high-powered scientific research laboratory. The reason is the same for both. Commercial business processes and frameworks make nonprofits more efficient in their operations, better at raising the money they need to operate, and better at dealing with the challenges of growth.

Over the last thirty years here in San Diego, we've seen the transformational power of bringing business professionals to the social sector. The boards of thirty years ago, filled with good but inexperienced people trying to do the right thing, have become tightly run nonprofits working toward specific and measurable goals and remaining focused and disciplined along the way. I don't know of any successful charities that don't run on business principles.

When I first entered the nonprofit world, I was surprised how naive people on boards could be. They had good hearts, but that often wasn't enough. Because of my background, I gravitated toward my fellow businesspeople on those boards.

Over time, I've changed my mind. I've learned to appreciate the importance of people with heart, commitment, and dedication. More than ever, I'm convinced that both types can successfully operate side by side. Frankly, they have to. Just as I would never want a board composed solely of do-gooders, I would also never serve on one filled with nothing but steely, bottom-line businesspeople.

As for myself, I've learned the value of humility. One of the biggest flaws of business professionals is that they come into the job believing that they know better than anyone else how things should run.

I consciously try not to put myself in such a lofty position. I don't claim to be an expert. I believe in bringing in attorneys, accountants, and other real experts to explain their roles; when it comes to searching for next the leader, I almost always recommend that we go to outside search firms. I like to deal with outside experts, and I try to teach my fellow board members, whatever their backgrounds, to feel the same way. There's usually a lot of business education that nonprofit people need—but there's also a lot of subtle things about the nonprofit world that businesspeople don't understand. We all need to be open to being taught something new.

One of the most important things I try to tell my nonbusiness fellow board members is about the notion of *continuity*. Charities tend to swing back and forth in search of money in an attempt to meet the changing needs of those they help.

While some evolution is fine, a nonprofit that allows itself to be whipsawed about usually ends up regretting it. From the first day I join a given board, I advocate for consistency in action and conservatism in mission.

For example, many boards only allow their members to have one-year terms. I almost always argue for a three-year term plus the potential for a one-time renewal. This enables the institution to get rid of nonperforming board members after not too long a tenure but also to retain those members who have reached the top of their learning curve and can really make a valuable contribution.

In other words, reappoint good directors and retire others gracefully, but give both time to prove themselves. On the other hand, don't allow even good people to stay on forever. As has been found with university presidents, if administrators' tenure exceeds the normal time frame, even the best ones will begin to coast.

By the same token, ensure that the institution sticks to its core product or service. That is the very heart of continuity.

I am a member of a San Diego nonprofit political group whose mission statement is to back candidates and laws that support the business community. Last year, this group decided to back a candidate but at the same time to actively attack another candidate who was also probusiness. I told them two things: First, I don't believe in being negative. Second, and more important, their actions violated their mission statement. I told them in no uncertain terms that the group had to either amend its mission statement or stop attacking that candidate.

Nonprofits will always tend to drift away from their mission statements, because the market, rather than disciplining their lack of focus, will reward that drift. Once it occurs, it will fall on the businesspeople on the board to hold the enterprise to its own rules and either rewrite the mission statement or get back to adhering to it.

Finally, *listen to the people.* In the end, nonprofits, and especially charities, are only as good as their volunteers and those they serve. Jim Collins isn't alone in teaching us that great enterprises in the public sector are led through consensus and persuasion, not by job title and fiat. I've learned a lot about this from a book called *Start-up Nation.* It's about how small, impoverished Israel became one of the most economically successful countries in the world—in large part because of the work of everyday people, not high-powered executives. Nowhere was this more the case than in the Israeli army—perhaps the most technologically advanced on the planet—where much of the development came from privates rather than generals.

After more than forty years in the social sector and having sat on uncounted boards, I believe more than ever in hearing people out, in not trying to run a charity strictly like a business, in the power of persuasion and consensus, and in trusting the ideas of people who truly care and have dedicated their lives to the institution and the people they serve.

We need to listen. To everyone. The secret to success can be hidden in the most unlikely places ... and in the most unlikely people.

CHAPTER 7

UNDERSTAND AND IDENTIFY POINTS OF LEVERAGE

In the mid-1980s, when I finally made the jump from part-time to full-time philanthropy, I set for myself two principles for conducting my new career:

1. *Delegate responsibility.* The world of charities and nonprofits is no different than the commercial world in this respect. The more you delegate your duties to others, the more you extend your reach, amplify your impact, and free yourself from minutiae to focus on larger, strategic concerns.

   Unfortunately, while that sounds good in principle, in practice it is much harder to maintain this philosophy in the social sector. This is the case for a number of reasons. For one thing, charities are almost always understaffed, and it's hard to delegate when there's nobody there to delegate to. Another reason is that because charities are often largely staffed by volunteers, you can't always be certain that the people you are delegating to—while they are no doubt good people—are capable of handling those tasks.

But most of all, the biggest impediment to delegation in a charity or nonprofit is *you*. The same seasoned executives, who in their commercial careers happily carved up their duties, assigned them to others, and then ruthlessly tracked the performance of those subordinates, will often find themselves leading or chairing a charity for which they are unwilling to do any of those things. They understandably become emotionally involved and averse to failure; they want to be involved in everything and want the program to be perfect.

This happens to almost everyone. After all, why would you devote this much time, energy, and money to a charity if you hadn't already fallen in love with the service it provides? I'm not suggesting that you should not care about the institution to which you have volunteered; I am suggesting instead that you constantly remind yourself that the charity will be better off only if you delegate your tasks and save yourself for the big challenges.

2. *Operate most at pivot points.* This is, of course, true for most enterprises. You make changes where they can have the maximum impact. But this strategy is particularly true in the social sector. There, because money is almost always short and the enterprises are perpetually understaffed, a broad approach to any challenge is usually impossible. In the world of charity, you simply can't be all things to all people. Moreover, your ability to scale up is also usually severely circumscribed. What you *can* do is precisely identify the projects, places, and people you can influence to have the maximum long-term effect.

    Once you have looked for pivot points where you intend to make changes and have made your commitment, you should look for those institutions (either already existing or that you must create) that you can leverage to create that change. It is a two-step process, which unfortunately even experienced philanthropists mistake as being just one step. If you create a product or service with one organization and fail to appreciate that it will take a different institution to roll it out to the target recipients, it will be as if it had never happened at all. All of your efforts will be for naught.

    Over the years I have added one more rule to these two:

3. *If you want to have impact, smaller is almost always better.* It is human nature to be attracted to established institutions that already dominate their field. After all, they have money, the top talent, and the glow of success. They instantly confer on you a higher profile and considerable social credit. Secretly, you also know that if you screw up, you likely won't much hurt that institution.

    But those advantages come at a cost. Experience has shown me that the big, successful charities and nonprofits are also much more likely to be bureaucratic, slow to change, and trapped by the weight of their own legacies. So it is often a better strategy to pick a small charity or group where you can have real impact as your vehicle for change.

These three rules have served me well over the last three decades. Though obviously they should never be hard and fast—life is much too complicated for that—I still regularly follow them whenever I've decided to get involved in a new project. Moreover, I regularly revisit them and compare them to my current work to make sure that I'm not getting complacent or drifting off track.

Having maximum leverage means having not only maximum control but also maximum flexibility and independence. And those last two, I'm convinced, are crucial to a satisfying and effective career.

• • •

Fortune, as they say, favors the bold. But the reality is that what outsiders may see as a high-risk venture may in fact be a comparatively safe investment if you have found a powerful point of leverage—the funding, the team, the market, an innovative strategy—that others have failed to discover.

In 1981, it became apparent to me that San Diego needed a new business bank. I developed a strategy to establish just such a bank, but before I went public with my plan, I lined up its potential president/CEO and a group of interested potential directors. This founding team agreed that San Diegans needed a hometown business lender.

Banking rules required that the size of any loan offered by a bank of this type could not exceed a certain percentage of the bank's net worth. That posed a problem because business loans are usually much larger than home loans. That meant that we needed to raise an initial starting capital much greater than a typical community bank.

Instead of letting this become a deal breaker, we decided to take the opposite approach; we chose to raise an unprecedented $15 million in beginning capital, which at that time was approximately *twice* the starting capital of any previous US bank. Some said that this was a risky move, but in fact we were oversubscribed. My team and I had done our homework, and we knew that what seemed to be a high-risk deal was in fact a very safe move.

The resulting First National Bank of San Diego was a success from the start—and remained so even after it was purchased twenty-five years later. It is now Pacific Western Bank, and it is still my personal bank.

Coming off the success of the bank, my team and I made another bold move: we decided to build a luxury hotel in Coronado, across the harbor from downtown San Diego. The perceived risk here was the competitive threat by the hotel's famous neighbor, the world-renowned Hotel del Coronado. This stately, architecturally famous property was the premier hotel for high-end guests and San Diego's most important conventions.

After learning that we had won the bid to lease the land from the San Diego Port District, the owner of the del Coronado embarked on a public campaign attacking our team's lack of experience. He even wrote to our proposed construction lender, suggesting it decline our construction loan.

What the del Coronado owner saw as our weakness was in fact our greatest strength. I had a brilliant team, and what they lacked in hotel experience they more than made up in business (especially real estate development) talent, boldness, and the willingness to see old problems in new ways.

In the end, we opened the Le Meridian Hotel in 1988 to rather high initial occupancy. Because our team members were principally developers rather than operators, we had no intention of actually running the hotel. Instead, we played to our strengths and sold the property in 1989 for $290,000 per room—at that time, a record hotel price for San Diego.

During the construction phase, my agitator wrote me a letter telling me that the hotel would be the biggest lemon of my career. Soon after our record sale was announced, I sent him a letter in return stating that our project produced some of the sweetest lemonade of my career.

Hot off of selling our hotel, we were ready for another challenging project. We assembled another small team to develop a major industrial park in the city of Poway, a neighboring community on the northeast side of San Diego. Here, the challenge would be moving earth, so we partnered with San Diego's largest road builder.

Starting with 480 gross acres, we shaved off the hilltops and filled in the ravines, which were up to two hundred feet in depth. All told, we moved and compacted just over twenty million cubic yards of earth—one of the largest earth-moving projects in San Diego County's history. Today, some twenty years later, the Poway Business Center is full of some of the San Diego region's finest companies, including the regional headquarters of GEICO, Allied Van Lines, Costco, and Home Depot.

Once again, by having the right team and identifying critical points of leverage, we had turned what could have been a high-risk project into a comparatively safe—and profitable—one.

• • •

In 2004, I received a telephone call from fellow real estate operator Bob Klein in Palo Alto. Bob had a crazy idea about floating a large, statewide bond issue to support stem-cell research. Crazy or not, by the end of the phone call, I knew that this was something I needed to investigate.

At that time, stem-cell research was comparatively controversial, with several states going so far as to ban such research—not least because at the time, it could only be done using fetal cells. The more investigation I did, the more I believed that such a program would not only benefit humankind but also greatly compliment the greater San Diego medical research scene.

So I signed on to Bob's team. Our task was to present and convince a majority of California voters to approve a $3 billion bond issue to underwrite stem-cell research on the November 2004 ballot.

My first step was to persuade the board of the Burnham Institute (as it was then still called) to publicly support this initiative. We were the first such institution in California—and the only nonprofit medical research institute in San Diego—to publicly support this initiative.

Needless to say, we didn't take this step without some reservations and a lot of internal debate. Sometimes leadership decisions can be both risky *and* important, but if you can't make such decisions, you shouldn't be in the job. In fact, you *want* to face such decisions, nerve-racking as they may be, because they often create the kind of leverage that is the key to major victories.

That November, the voters of California approved Klein's bond proposition. Now it was time to get organized for the future.

The La Jolla Mesa region of San Diego is home to four of the world's leading medical research institutes, all located within walking and/or bicycling distance of each other. That fact, to my mind, presented another leverage opportunity. Soon after the proposition's approval, I led the formation of the first ever medical consortium for stem-cell research composed of Burnham Institute, Scripps Research, Salk Institute, and UCSD Medical. Together we set out to gain a piece of the new bond.

According to its approved terms, ten percent of the new bond money was earmarked for brick-and-mortar grants. The largest individual grant was to be $50 million and required 20 percent in philanthropic dollars on top of the state's money. In other words, to get money we first had to raise money.

I knew exactly where to go: to my then-new partner and friend in philanthropy, Denny Sanford. Denny had already shown his commitment to bioresearch by adding his name to mine, along with a $50-million contribution, at the institute. Now I was asking for even more.

Denny was particularly motivated to help San Diego after his home state, North Dakota, voted against conducting any stem-cell research. He agreed to a $30-million gift for what would be titled the Sanford Consortium for Regenerative Medicine.

Photo credit: Jason A. Knowles

Designed by Fentress Architects, the Sanford Consortium for Regenerative Medicine works to expand collaborative stem cell research and translate discoveries into clinical therapies and cures.

In 2011, the La Jolla Institute for Allergy and Immunology joined the consortium as its fifth and equal member. Today we are the most prominent consortium for stem-cell research in the world, and it all happened because Bob Klein spotted an opportunity and used the leverage of his phone list to make the idea real—and because I did the same thing for the biotech industry of San Diego.

There's one more point of leverage in this story. Seeing the promising early results of the new research, eight years later Denny decided to maximize that leverage by going all in. In early 2014, the Sanford Stem Cell Clinical Center at UC San Diego Health was born to continue the progress of all the work described above. With $100 million of underwriting, this truly first-of-a-kind center is adding to what Bob Klein's phone call was all about eleven years ago.

Roberta, the family, and me at the 1996 renaming of the
La Jolla Cancer Research Foundation.

As I look back at the transformation of the LJCRF into the Burnham Institute, then the Sanford Burnham Medical Research Institute, and now the Sanford Burnham Prebys Medical Discovery Institute—not to mention the creation of the Sanford Consortium for Regenerative Medicine and the Sanford Stem Cell Clinical Center at UC San Diego Health— what I see is a twenty-year string of leverage points, each identifying a unique opportunity to improve on the status quo, build something five or ten times larger, and to do that again and again.

None of these actions—a phone call, a casual conversation, and a tour—were momentous in and of themselves. But they were each precisely timed and targeted for the maximum impact, and they were executed with a certain amount of guts. It's not easy to ask anyone, even a very wealthy person, to write a check for millions of dollars, devote years of their life, or bet their reputation on what is often little more than a notion on your part.

Moreover, the consequences of that "ask," as casually as it may have been delivered, can be enormous. In the short term, the potential donor may not just say no; they might resent the very fact that you did ask and took advantage of your friendship. In the long term, should the project fail and those millions be wasted, it may cost you that friendship; you may never be forgiven.

That's a big reason why I never ask anyone to give to a charity or institution to which I haven't already made a donation of money and/or time. I make the donation not just to prove to other donors that I am committed to that project—though that is certainly part of it—but rather because I can't ask anyone to give part of their hard-earned fortune to an initiative that I am not already deeply a part of, have helped design to my own satisfaction, and have been involved with long enough to fully know its strengths and weaknesses. I don't just want to show these potential donors that I have skin in the game; I want them to see that my heart and brain are committed to it, as well.

• • •

I had a role in the creation of another entity: the Rady School of Management at UCSD. Once again, it had the smallest and humblest of beginnings, but through a series of leverages, it became something quite magnificent.

It all started in 2002, in a parking lot in an industrial neighborhood. Four of us were standing around debriefing after a meeting we had just attended in a nearby building. The topic of the meeting was UCSD's approaching fortieth anniversary. The question we asked ourselves was: How can we better connect UCSD with San Diego's economy?

We all agreed that the university and the city shared two major attributes: high-tech commerce and innovation. With that in mind, what might be the best bridge between them? After several other suggestions had been made, someone suggested starting a graduate business school concentrating precisely on "high-tech commerce and innovation." We all decided that this could be the perfect model.

We took the concept to UCSD Chancellor Robert Dynes. He was intrigued and asked us to "write it up." It was in shaping this proposal that we came up with the crucial differentiator between this proposed new business school and the many other business schools in southern California and the Southwest. We would target a potential student body largely composed of individuals who had already earned science degrees. We believed that this would greatly increase our chances of producing graduates who would go to work in high-tech commerce and innovation and stay and contribute to the San Diego economy rather than leaving the area to pursue careers on Wall Street or in consulting.

As it turns out, we made the right decision. Today, just over 80 percent of Rady Business School's students enter with science degrees, and nearly all graduate and return to their fields. Better yet, here's the real proof of the results: in Rady's first ten years, its students and graduates started a total of seventy start-up companies. Meanwhile, Rady's ratings have soared in the national business school rankings. All this came from a quick conversation in a parking lot.

• • •

I will share a final story about leverage and how it can also carry considerable risk.

By law, charities and nonprofits are limited in how involved they can get with politics and advocacy. If they go too far, they risk losing their tax exemption, and that can be catastrophic. For good reason, they are wary of participating in anything that smacks of politics and elections.

As you'll remember from earlier in this chapter, my involvement with the California stem-cell initiative began with that phone call from Bob Klein. At that time I was chairman of the Burnham Institute, but Bob called me because we were old compatriots from the real estate industry.

Nevertheless, when Bob told me what he was doing, I resolved not only to help him personally—and indeed, I ended up helping him write Proposition 71 (the California Stem Cell Research and Cures Act), getting it on the ballot, and heading the team promoting it—but to also get the Burnham Institute involved in any way I could.

Needless to say, this added a lot more risk to my involvement. It was one thing for Malin Burnham, private citizen who happened to chair a medical research institute, to get involved with a controversial voter initiative. It was a whole different matter to put the reputation and weight of the institute itself behind this campaign.

But I was convinced it was the right thing to do. Bob Klein asked if the Burnham Institute would come out in support of the measure, and I went in front of the board and argued that we do so—even though the institute had never done anything like this before. We might be setting a dangerous precedent, and we risked being pulled into one of the biggest scientific and political controversies of the era.

Admitting all of those risks, I nevertheless told the board that I thought this was the time to take a stand. Our support might go a long way to helping create the only state-backed stem-cell initiative in the world—a massive research project that could profoundly affect humankind and transform both San Diego and the Burnham Institute in the process.

In the end, the board voted to publicly endorse California State Proposition 71, as it was then designated. As we all know, it passed. It has fulfilled everything we expected from it and more. It also turned out that the Burnham Institute was the only medical nonprofit in San Diego and the first in the entire state of California to endorse the bill. That, to me, was real leadership.

For me, it was another lesson in the power of leverage. I could have chosen to run around and gather up endorsements for Proposition 71 from a score of noted scientists, doctors, and businesspeople in the San Diego community. That's how it is usually done. But in my gut I knew that this time, it would take the full reputation of the Burnham Institute—not just a list of influential names—to convince the public of the seriousness of the cause.

It often comes down to the culture of an institution when deciding where and when to apply leverage. Would I risk the institute's reputation and tax exemption again on a political campaign? Probably not—but I won't say "never" until I see the cause. There is no fixed formula for doing this.

• • •

When we speak of leverage, we tend to see it as an action: the application of influence at the precise point and moment when it can have the greatest effect. But you can also look at leverage in a different way. Ultimately, the real leverage points are, in fact, *people.* The real source of the Rady School of Business was not just the conversation between the four of us in the parking lot, nor the crucial decision to orient the school toward science and innovation, but the willingness of the four of us to get engaged, to pursue the concept, and to fight to make it real. Points of leverage only succeed because someone is there to *move the lever.*

That brings us back to where we were when we began this chapter. Sometimes you discover that *you* are the point of leverage. In those moments, you find yourself having to make a major decision. I began by telling you that one of my rules is to always try to delegate authority; that's why I rarely assume the role of chairman and why I am always a strong advocate of hiring the best possible CEO. When, for example, the USS

Midway was moved to San Diego and I was asked to be part of the fund-raising committee for the move, I was more than happy to take a role supporting the individual who had successfully advocated for it.

But sometimes, for the good of the organization, you need to step in and assume leadership. This should never be done without a lot of reflection and consideration. When you realize that you are the real point of leverage for that organization's success, you have to act for the good of everyone.

How do you know that you are right in making this move? Once again, there is no formula. You have to listen to your gut, to that little voice inside you … and trust what it says.

CHAPTER 8

TAKING CHARGE

As you may have noticed, as a rule I prefer not to be the person in charge, the person in the limelight, the individual ultimately responsible for every decision. You may have also noticed that I've violated that rule on several occasions.

In all of the charities and nonprofits with which I am involved, my philosophy has always been that it is far better to have a man or woman with a full-time commitment and expertise in the field in the top job while I stay in the background, lending my skills and experience whenever I think it is valuable.

This strategy usually works. But sometimes, as we saw in chapter 6 with the leadership crisis at the San Diego YMCA, I've had to step forward and briefly assume leadership. Those moments don't come frequently; if they do, you need to question your own judgment. But they do come, so you must always be prepared to take leadership on a moment's notice, even if you are not in charge.

The good news is that charities and other nonprofits are typically run by very good and competent people. The bad

news is that they often lack the larger business sense and experience that comes from a successful career in the commercial
world. For that reason, there may be moments when the best
thing you can do to improve that institution's chances for
long-term success is to assume a temporary role of leading
the organization through its current crisis, often behind the
scenes and through the existing staff. Crucial to this temporary
"takeover" (because that is how it will be seen by some) is to set
a duration and benchmarks to returning control, to treat those
whose duties you have assumed with respect, and ultimately to
empower those managers, not coerce them, and mentor them
to be better at what they do.

• • •

Sometimes you need to take charge in order to cut through
a static or sluggish bureaucracy. This often happens when an
organization considers stepping beyond its traditional bound-
aries and doesn't know whether it is allowed to or who will take
responsibility if they are wrong. In this scenario, it is often best
not to tackle the challenge through a committee but instead
to lead the charge personally. Of course, if the initiative fails,
you alone will be blamed. But that's part of the excitement of
philanthropy.

A perfect example of this in my career took place at SDSU
back in 2000. SDSU is San Diego's oldest and largest public
university, but it didn't possess a freestanding residence for its
president.

Now, most important universities have residences for their presidents. In San Diego, both UCSD and USD have residences for their presidents. Of course, Stanford and Berkeley have them as well. These homes are more than just private residences. They also serve a major public function: they operate as a discreet interview location, a social gathering place, a reception site for VIPs, and a site for a myriad of other university and community activities. Yet somehow through the decades, SDSU never got around to providing such a facility to its presidents.

It was then-new President Steve Weber who decided to do something about this deficiency. I knew him but not well. He called me one day out of the blue and said that SDSU was being offered the donation of a mansion-sized residence in the town of Coronado. What if it were to be converted into a president's residence?

We could have organized an exploratory committee to investigate the opportunity, but by then too many wheels would have turned, and likely there would be no going back. So I simply cut through the process and told President Weber, "No, no, it's twelve miles from campus. The house is too far away to turn into a president's residence."

After I got off the phone, I realized that this was the first time any president of SDSU had ever mentioned the idea of such a residence to me. I also realized that they didn't need a committee to find such a building. After all, thinking like a veteran real estate man, the choice of location, available parking, and square footage were pretty circumscribed. The number of possible housing options would be very small, and the time to make a decision would probably be very short—so why not just do it myself?

I called back President Weber and said, "Let me help you."

Steve suggested appointing a house search committee. "No, Steve," I said. "Let me quietly do some investigation, since real estate has been my career." I then drew up a list of required attributes:

- no more than a ten-minute drive from campus
- private, with a preference for a gated community
- ample parking
- enough space to accommodate groups of as many as 250 people
- a floor plan that allowed the family to be in their quarters while the president was acting as host in another part of the property

I predicted that it would take six to twelve months to find the right fit. It didn't take nearly that long. In fact, I found the perfect candidate literally next door to the campus. It was in a gated community of about fifty homes—not the most expensive development in San Diego but well qualified for its planned duty.

I knew several residential realtors in that area. To keep from spooking the market and boosting the price, I quietly confided in these realtors about what I was looking for and asked them to keep an eye out.

In the end, we looked at a total of six homes and toured President Weber through half of them. None really worked out. But as with many things, patience is a virtue in real estate. Finally, another house came on the market, and this one struck me as perfect in terms of location, size, style, and all of the other attributes the university was looking for.

It was the perfect house. By this point, we were several months into our search. Either we make this deal, I thought to myself, or I've got better things to do. I made the presentation. And to the relief of both of us, President Weber liked it enough to take his associates on a tour. They liked the place as well. It was time to make an offer.

Then we got another surprise: it turned out that SDSU was not in a financial position to buy the house we had selected. Worse, even if we managed to get the house gifted to the school, SDSU could still not accept it if there was a loan of any size attached to it.

This was singularly frustrating. We had the ideal property; even had an owner anxious to sell quickly. Because there would be no commission involved, the seller agreed to my price, but with the stipulation that we needed to close escrow in thirty days.

I wasn't sure I could raise the money that quickly. In the end, after a brief bit of soul-searching, I did the only thing I could: I put up the down payment money myself and bought the house, confident that I could raise the rest of the money. Because the university couldn't be involved with the deal, I negotiated the purchase in my own name. The deal was closed with my down payment and a six-month note.

That decision had an unexpected and funny side effect. It turns out that all of the largest home purchases in the area are officially reported in the *San Diego Daily Transcript*. After the closing of the house, the purchase—with my name attached to it—appeared in the *Transcript*. It wasn't long before a rumor was going around that Roberta and I were getting a divorce and that I was moving out into a new bachelor home! I couldn't even correct the rumor until the deal was officially gifted to SDSU.

Over the next few months, we collected the rest of the money, paid off the loan, and turned the house over to SDSU. Looking back, I'm more convinced than ever that this initiative could not have been accomplished by a committee, especially in such a short time window. Someone had to take charge—and in this case, it was me.

• • •

The Kyoto Prize is given annually "to those who have contributed significantly to the scientific, cultural, and spiritual betterment of mankind." The prize, which is awarded each November tenth, is given to a recipient in each of three categories: Advanced Technology, Basic Sciences, and Arts and Philosophy. Many consider the Kyoto second only to the Nobel Prize for international accomplishment.

Other than the Kyoto award ceremony, the only annual Kyoto Prize event is its annual symposium, which features the current laureates and is held in San Diego each spring. The program began in 2002 and very nearly died two years later. Therein lies another story about taking charge at the appropriate moment.

In 2004, a friend approached me and asked if I would help him put on a gala. "I don't put on galas," was my reply. But he was insistent that the committee to which he belonged desperately needed to build up the importance of the then two-year-old symposium, and in particular of the gala dinner that kicked off the event.

I said, "What exactly is the Kyoto Prize?" This was the depth of my ignorance on the subject.

I soon learned that San Diego had been selected as the host of the symposium two years before. Despite two comparatively successful annual events, the organizing committee had failed to achieve any real traction for the program in the public eye. San Diego was now at risk of losing its sponsorship of the Kyoto Prize Symposium unless it figured out how to give the event much greater prominence, including raising attendance at all three days of open, free conferences with the laureates and, of course, capturing the expected local, national, and international press coverage.

I agreed to get involved, not just because of my commitment to San Diego but also because USD was the academic cosponsor of the event.

Part of leadership is not just looking at what things are being done wrong but also determining what things are not being done at all. I quickly seized upon the idea of implementing two "interest generators."

First, I proposed that at our opening gala we present six $10,000, first-year college scholarships to high school seniors. In the international spirit of the Kyoto Prize, the scholarships would go to three students on each side of the San Diego–Tijuana border. These recipients would represent our region's potential future entrepreneurs and be a major part of the gala program.

Second, I proposed bringing in SDSU and UCSD as additional conference presentation hosts alongside USD. Initially it felt like I was walking on eggs by taking two-thirds of the laureate hosting away from USD, the school with which I was most intimately involved.

It turned out that USD was relieved by my decision. It was already weary of carrying the entire load of planning and promoting such a major international event. Now three major universities and nearly fifty thousand total students were involved, and we had access to three times as many venues in multiple locations. With the implementation of the major scholarship program, we were capturing the attention of high school students within more than a fifty-mile radius and in two countries, and the media was now calling. At last, we had the kind of high-profile event that the Kyoto Prize Symposium deserved.

More than a decade later, the Kyoto Prize Symposium is a major annual event on San Diego's calendar that draws large crowds and considerable media attention—not least for its scholarship awards. There has been a wonderful secondary effect: you can read the remarkable story of Rodrigo Ortega, one of those scholarship recipients, in chapter 5. I like to think that we now not only celebrate the great achievers of the present but that we also help create their counterparts of the future.

• • •

I'll finish this chapter as I began: be prepared to lead, even if you are not in charge. This is true not just in your professional life but in your personal life as well. In fact, that philosophy might just save your life.

About twelve years ago, Roberta and I and three other couples had just completed a delightful twelve-day private safari in Kenya. Now we were all heading for a four-day deluxe stay on one of the smaller islands of the Seychelles.

All air flights to and from the Seychelles land at the main capital island of Mahé. From there you transfer to your destination island via either a small ferry or a helicopter. We signed up to go out on the ferry and return on the helicopter.

As it turned out, our "ferry" was a well-worn, twenty-five-year-old, sixty-foot power yacht with a crew of three. The trip would be a one-hour, open-ocean transit. Even with good weather, neither the ship nor the trip seemed promising.

That was just the start. During the voyage the wind kept increasing, which made the trip increasingly uncomfortable. Even worse, when we arrived at our destination, there was no protective harbor or landing. Our ferry crew put down the anchor and launched an eight-foot rubber boat with an outboard engine. This was the craft designed to carry us and our baggage to shore. It was obvious to me that this rubber dingy was entirely too unstable to take all of us to shore.

That's when I decided to take control.

After all, I was a veteran of many more high-risk ocean experiences than any of our ferry crew, including the disastrous 1979 Fastnet race in which fifteen people drowned and thirty-two boats sank. Commandeering the ferry's ship-to-shore radio, I contacted the port and arranged for the resort team to transfer our party to shore with one of their larger—and much more stable—launch boats. We reached the shore safely and no worse for wear. I still shudder when I think what might have happened if we had attempted that voyage in the rubber boat.

Would I have done these things—take command, ruffle feathers, and make quick decisions—when I was younger? In all candor, *no.* Looking back, I don't think I became a "take charge" kind of person until I was nearly forty. It wasn't just my own emotional development and maturity at that age but also the fact that I had built up enough history of performance in both the for-profit and nonprofit worlds. People actually *listened* to me.

Beyond that, my confidence had grown during the preceding years with each success. I now trusted my wisdom and skills enough to stick my neck out, take responsibility, and if necessary, go to battle.

Of course, if that kind of confidence grows too great, it can be your worst enemy. You stop listening, you come to conclusions prematurely, and you tend to take too much control and too much credit. So even as my reputation grew, I constantly reminded myself that I *wasn't* the expert in everything, that others might have more relevant experience to the problem at hand, and most of all that I should lead by consensus whenever possible.

One trick I learned to reinforce this behavior was to share and discuss ideas rather than immediately implementing them—this allowed me to see if consensus grew around any of them. Sometimes it didn't. Sometimes I even got talked out of my own ideas. That was good because not only did it keep my ego in check, but the result was almost always a better idea. In the end, it is all about community before self.

Now that I'm nearly in my ninth decade, I find myself in a position of considerable respect, earned through my many years of service. This respect can be quite humbling. I don't tell most people that one reason I hold the position I do in the San Diego community is that I haven't had that much competition for the leadership role.

There aren't many people who do what I do. Sure, there are a lot of good folks who devote themselves to one charity or another. My style has been to involve myself in numerous charities and nonprofits across multiple fields but to rarely take the helm in any of them. That way I can cover more territory, and my ideas can be common to several organizations at the same time.

Needless to say, this also adds to my responsibilities. It's one thing to throw out ideas when few people are listening and you'll have little responsibility over the result. It's a lot different when you speak and everyone at the table turns to listen and you know that you will lead the resulting initiative—and take the blame if it fails.

There's a burden and a risk to being the person people listen to. I remember leading the group to buy the city's premier newspaper, the *San Diego Union*, and convert it to nonprofit ownership. Over the eighteen months of that negotiation, I regularly had strangers come up to me on the street, shake my hand, and say, "I sure hope you can buy that newspaper." It's a long way from selling apartment buildings. But I look on the bright side: It is precisely because people listen to me—and because it is human nature that some people, because of my position, want me to fail—that I have been forced over the years to smooth down my rough edges, be deliberate, and most of all, be serious. And those were good traits for me to learn.

The evolution of my career reached a kind of milestone when I was approached by the deans of the UCSD medical school and its Rady School of Management. Over dinner they asked me a simple but profound question: Did I think that the San Diego community had the potential to become *the* medical center of the southwest United States?

"Why come to me?" I asked them. They replied that they believed I might be able to take leadership on such a giant and far-reaching initiative. I was enormously flattered—after all, I was being asked to lead perhaps the greatest transformation yet of the city I loved. It was also an enormous gesture of trust by these distinguished figures. And I knew that I had now reached the point in my career and experience when I could entertain such an offer—or even welcome it.

It wasn't long before I called together the heads of four of San Diego's biggest health centers—with revenues of $2 billion plus each—to discuss how they could work together to provide full-spectrum services to the region's growing ranks of "medical tourists" and become the health magnet for ten western states.

We have just begun this initiative, but we are already well on our way to regional leadership. Twenty years ago, I would have found the very idea of taking charge of such a project daunting. Now, I have no doubt we will succeed or that I'm comfortable being the leader to do it.

And I can't wait to get there.

CHAPTER 9

CONTROVERSY AND UNEXPECTED SUCCESS

A lesson about philanthropy that took me years to learn and is now getting considerable attention in a very different field is the power of the *platform*.

The electronics industry, especially social networking companies like Facebook, have learned that success often comes by creating the setting and supplying the tools to make other people realize their dreams. Once engaged, the combined intelligence, talent, experience, and energy of this volunteer army will accomplish far more than you ever could alone.

I learned this lesson beginning in 1993 with the aircraft carrier USS *Midway*.

It all began with a phone call from Bob Lichter, an old friend and former associate of mine at Burnham Real Estate. Bob explained to me that there was an individual named Alan Uke who had a crazy idea about berthing the *Midway* in San Diego harbor as a floating museum and classroom. "I don't know anything about the harbor," Bob said, "but you do. Would you be willing to talk to him?"

The USS Midway Museum, one of San Diego's top attractions, drawing over 1.3 million visitors a year. I played a pivotal role in "borrowing" it from the US Navy and moving it to San Diego.

I agreed, though not without trepidation. I knew a little about berthing retired Navy ships, and what I knew wasn't very positive. In terms of revenues, aircraft carriers weren't as bad as battleships, but even so, they were not very successful. Of the four retired carriers berthed around the country—the *Intrepid* in New York City; the *Hornet* in Alameda, California; the *Lexington* in Corpus Christi, Texas; and the *Yorktown* in Mount Pleasant, South Carolina—none had been able to operate in the black. Though the *Midway* obviously had a great name, it had gone into service in 1945 and had never seen combat like the *Yorktown*, nor picked up Gemini and Apollo astronauts like the *Hornet*. The *Midway*'s claim to fame largely rested on its work during rescue missions in the Philippines and Haiti.

I knew from experience that any major installation or construction within one thousand feet of the harbor required the approval of the California Coastal Commission, which would inevitably look askance at everything about a giant aircraft carrier—from the view of the wetlands it would obstruct to the effect of its shadow on harbor sea life.

I also knew that such a project had several things going for it, not least that San Diego is a true Navy town that would no doubt embrace the addition of such a noble ship. On top of that, I figured we could get the *Midway* pretty cheaply, as it was mothballed in Bremerton, Washington, and likely doomed otherwise to scrap. Most of the costs would not be for the ship but for the surrounding infrastructure. In terms of added square footage, that made it a bargain.

But most of all, I sensed that given the unique nature of our city, San Diego would be able to make use of the *Midway* in ways nobody had yet imagined. Little did I know…

A few days later I found myself meeting with Alan Uke. I chose to hold the meeting in my office because it had an unobstructed view of the entire San Diego harbor, which I thought would help us both with visualization. Uke rolled out a chart of the harbor and pointed out the window at a particular location.

"It won't fit," I told him. "I've been sailing that harbor for sixty years, and there's no way a ship of that size will fit in that location. Instead," I swung my finger across the chart, "it should be *here*." The chart showed three piers next to downtown San Diego, the furthest one called "Navy Pier." I told him that the ship would fit on the far side of that structure; moreover, there was room for parking and for getting equipment on and off the carrier. Eleven years later, that was exactly where the *Midway* was berthed and where it remains to this day.

I decided to get involved. It would prove to be a multistep process. First I had to assemble a small team. Together we would raise money for the initial engineering work, environmental studies, and early promotion, and we would ultimately develop a long-term fund-raising strategy for the entire project. Riskiest of all, we had to do all of this long before there was any assurance that the Pentagon and the US Navy would ever let us have the USS *Midway*. Luckily, we knew that we could reduce that risk somewhat with the help of Alan Uke; his company made underwater cameras and surveillance equipment, which gave him excellent contacts in the Navy.

Meanwhile, on the promise of the carrier coming, we raised $2.25 million. It wasn't easy; the money came mostly in small chunks, and raising it required some clever marketing. For example, in the Navy, a "centarian" is a pilot who has landed successfully on a carrier at sea one hundred times. So we created a Centarian Founders group to which donors could join for a $20,000 donation.

But this initial tranche of money wasn't nearly enough. Navy Pier needed a major rebuild, including the replacement of scores of rotting piles, if it was going to be able to withstand the pull of a massive ship tied to it, not to mention the weight of support trucks and thousands of visitors. Meanwhile, we would have to purchase wetlands in the harbor covering *three times* the shadow of the *Midway*.

So I went to the bank and took out a loan for $3.25 million. I secured the loan by asking a number of my friends to guarantee $250,000 each, and I would pick up any shortfall. With that personal motivation, I was successful in finding all the necessary backers.

So far, so good. But now we had the challenge of the Coastal Commission. As I said, it had jurisdiction over anything within one thousand feet of the coast, and the Navy Pier and parking lots certainly fell within that range. The commission didn't waste any time: soon after we announced our intentions, they came out publically against it, claiming that the *Midway* would unacceptably block the view of the water.

We could have responded immediately; that's the usual strategy. Instead, we decided to wait. We now knew that we had a battle on our hands, and we decided to fight it on our own battlefield.

Most members of the commission are local politicians in their own areas of the state: city council people, county supervisors, and other local operators. The commission meets every other month, rotating up and down the state. We decided to wait until it came to San Diego, and when it did, we filled the hall with our strongest supporters. This surprised the commissioners. But the crowning moment came when someone from our side stood up and announced, "Ladies and gentlemen of the commission, the *Midway* won't block the view; it will *be the view!*" The applause was overwhelming.

The Coastal Commission voted unanimously in our favor.

Not quite all our tribulations were behind us. We had managed to raise millions of dollars and had run the gauntlet of gathering local and state support, but we still didn't have the USS *Midway*! Alan Uke's connections had proved quite useful, but they only got us in the door at the Pentagon. What we didn't anticipate was the astonishingly glacial pace of the federal bureaucracy. On several occasions we thought we had final approval in place only to have a change in command occur at the Department of the Navy, whereupon we had to start over again almost from the beginning.

In the end, it took *eleven years* for our team to finally get a letter of commitment from the Navy allowing us to take possession of the *Midway*.

By then, much had changed. Alan Uke now largely advised the project from the sidelines. Meanwhile, as the likelihood of getting approval for the *Midway* increased, so did the number of volunteers. By the time approval came, the board of directors for the project had grown to forty-five people, with an executive committee of sixteen. As for myself, I was a member of the board but never went to board meetings. Seeing a crisis pending with a swollen board unable to make quick and crisp decisions, the board voted to create a small committee to restructure its leadership. That committee came to my office in June 2004.

The delegation explained to me that it was proposing to reduce the board from forty-five members to just twenty-five—moving the rest into an ex officio role—and shrinking the executive committee to just seven members. I told them it was a great idea. "Thank you," they replied, "but here's our concern: if we do this restructuring improperly, there may be a riot. So we need your help. We'd like for you to be our new chairman of the board."

"Whoa," I replied. "Wait a minute. This is all coming too fast."

In the end, I did accept the chairmanship—but not before the board agreed to my strategy for dealing with the restructuring. As I guessed, they already had a list of people whom they wanted on and off the new board. I told them that this was the wrong approach. Instead, I insisted that they draw up a list of fifteen or more attributes they wanted in directors—i.e., a banker, an attorney, a retired military flag officer, a marketing person, and so on.

"Now," I said, "go down that list and fill each of those boxes with a name." The actual process of filling in the boxes was straightforward; now that we understood what we wanted for a board, it was obvious who belonged on it.

While I'm sure there were some hurt feelings in the end, the fact is that we never heard one criticism of how the selection was done. That was pretty amazing, and after forty years in business, I had just learned another lesson in life: people want to win, but just as important, they want the process to be fair. And that's what we gave them.

Now we had an aircraft carrier to deal with—and not much time. Once we got our letter of commitment, we set to work. First, the *Midway* had to be taken out of mothballs in Bremerton and towed to the Naval Air Station in Alameda,

California. There, it got a new exterior paint job and was prepared for shipping to San Diego. The final leg took place in January 2004, and the ship was temporarily berthed on the Navy side of the San Diego Bay, just five hundred yards from its eventual home on Navy Pier. Its presence just five hundred yards away served as an added prod for us to get our side of the bay ready—not that we needed one.

The very day the letter arrived we launched a frenzy of activity. We quickly set up multiple teams to plan the parking lot, the support structures, and the stairs from pier to ship, as we could hardly make visitors climb up rope ladders. We also cleaned up all the debris on Navy Pier and set to work replacing any rotted pilings. Then we repaved the pier.

The USS *Midway* was officially opened to the public on June 7, 2004. But that was just the beginning. While much of the San Diego community met the arrival of the carrier with open arms, others were less welcoming. Their biggest concern was that the ship would prove to be a white elephant and that after the initial hoopla, it would become a perpetual drain on the city's coffers.

Even before we got the *Midway*, I remember getting a call from a reporter at the *San Diego Union*. "Look," he said, "I know you're working hard to get the *Midway*. But I've got to tell you that if you do get it, it is liable to be the worst mistake of your life. I cover all the museums in the San Diego area. I know all their attendance numbers. You estimate that you'll get 400,000 visitors per year. Well, I'm telling you that you'll never get that many. This project is bound to fail."

Luckily I had anticipated just such a call. We had hired a research firm to give us an estimate on attendance, and they had predicted we'd see 600,000 visitors. We wanted to be conservative about it, so we set our break-even goal at just 400,000. "I'm confident we'll reach that number," I told him. When we hung up, I knew that the reporter still believed we were destined to fail and that the *Midway* would hurt the city in the process.

In fact, in our opening year, the *Midway* drew nearly 800,000 attendees including a large number of international visitors, notably from China and Japan. As I write this, we expect 1.2 million visitors this year. We have succeeded beyond our dreams. Why? For four reasons, each of them another lesson about successful charities and nonprofits.

First, we kept our ticket price very low—typically less than $20 per person. When you compare that to the city's two other biggest tourist attractions—$40 per ticket at the San Diego Zoo and $70 plus parking at Sea World—you can see why budget-minded visitors and locals looking for an inexpensive day out might choose the *Midway*.

Second, the *Midway* has succeeded for a reason I've known since the beginning of my real estate career. As realtors famously say, the three most important features of property are location, location, and location. Even more than the *Intrepid*, with its berth on the East River in Manhattan, the USS *Midway* has the best historic ship berth in the United States—certainly better than the other carriers. It is almost impossible to enter downtown San Diego without driving past its enormous and appealing form. Picking Navy Pier over any other location on the bay proved a critical decision.

The third reason was opportunity. When we sat down and pondered the number of revenue-producing ways the *Midway* might be used, we came up with a total of a dozen. Most of them were related to two programs: daytime visitor tours and occasional, mostly corporate, evening events. After all, those were the key revenue sources for our counterparts in other cities.

But because of our location and our accessibility, we discovered something already learned by young entrepreneurs in Silicon Valley building social networking sites: create an appealing venue and the right tools, and your users will come up with their own solutions. The *Midway* was a blank slate, a tabula rasa upon which San Diegans could write their own stories and come up with their own events, and we had the staff and equipment to help them make those dreams come true.

The results came quickly. Just a few months after we opened, I got a call from our CEO, a retired two-star admiral. "I've got the McMillin family," he said, "all three generations of them in San Diego, and they want to hold Corky McMillin's funeral on board the *Midway*. They need two thousand seats on the flight deck, composed so that the central control island is behind the stage, with seating for important local figures. Can we do it?"

Of course we could—and did. The success of that day soon led to our hosting other ceremonies including corporate events, civic events, entertainment, and events of every kind for as many as four thousand people each. Most compelling and unexpected of all is that about every ninety days, the flight deck hosts US government citizenship ceremonies, often for more than one thousand new Americans and their families. As you can imagine, an aircraft carrier is a hugely patriotic venue for such an event—very different from a church or hall—and those ceremonies are immensely popular.

Once we realized what we had, we set out to create our own events. The most successful to date is our annual gala fund-raising event. Each year in late August it attracts a full crowd to watch fireworks, Marines jumping out of helicopters onto the flight deck, and a host of other patriotic activities. For that event we also created the *Midway* American Patriot Award. Its first recipient was Bob Hope, who had performed two of his legendary Christmas shows for troops on board the *Midway*. Subsequent recipients have included astronauts and Lee Iacocca, whom we honored for his restoration of the Statue of Liberty. For that event we called ourselves the West Coast equivalent of the Statue of Liberty. I was hugely honored in 2013 to receive the award myself; I'm the only native San Diegan to receive it to date.

One of our biggest surprises has been the *Midway's* school program. Other ships offer tours for students, but we go all the way. We host day-long, free programs giving schoolchildren tours of the historic ship and science, technology, engineering, and mathematics (STEM) programs for entire classrooms. Every year, more than fifty thousand schoolchildren attend this program, with six thousand spending the night on board (with chaperones). Many kids say it is the best experience of their school year.

And that's only the start. We have now created a virtual STEM program, weaving in themes related to both the ship and patriotism. It is available to students all around the nation. We expect to eventually exceed a million kids per year in this program.

As I said, we began with a list of a dozen possible public uses of the *Midway*; we now regularly manage more than *thirty* different programs. The lesson we've learned is that in this fast-paced, modern world, you can't predict how people will use what you offer. The best thing you can do is empower them to come up with their own novel applications.

The fourth and biggest lesson of the *Midway* project is the power of volunteers. During the planning for the project, I often heard talk about the importance of docents. I didn't pay it much attention. To me, docents were volunteers who stood silently in the doorway of art galleries and museums and waited for visitors to ask them how to find the bathroom. I could not have been more wrong. Our docents and volunteers are the absolute backbone of the *Midway's* operations and are the single most critical reason for our success.

San Diego has the most densely populated military instal-lations in the United States, with forty thousand Marines at Camp Pendleton and thousands more Navy and Naval Aviation personnel stationed within the county. Add to that the hundreds of thousands of military personnel and their families who have retired to the region, and you have the greatest concentration of veterans in the country.

This population and its enthusiasm for all things military played a big role in my decision to join the *Midway* project. We counted on them to be regular visitors to the carrier. What I didn't count on was that this population would also provide our program with a small army of volunteers willing to do everything from greeting visitors in the parking lot and escorting them aboard to teaching classes and adapting the ship to make it more visitor friendly. Others donate time at our nearby hangar at the Naval Air Station, repairing our collection of vintage aircraft. Each day, seventy docents and volunteers out of a total of more than three hundred arrive in the morning, cheerful and anxious to devote their day to the ship—and it shows.

These people are not only dedicated; they are also wonderful representatives of the *Midway*. We regularly conduct exit reviews with our visitors, and docents are always at the top of the list of positive comments. I can truly say that they are the key to our success. Their hard work and commitment is ultimately what distinguishes us from other historic ships around the country.

The USS *Midway* has proven to be a great asset to San Diego. It has taught me great lessons about organizing large-scale projects around people who truly care. One of those people is Alan Uke. His bust now stands at the entrance to the *Midway*, giving proper credit to the man who started it all.

As for me, I'm still not done with the *Midway*. I have one more challenge. The carrier may be operating at a profit now, but mighty warships are surprisingly fragile to the vagaries of seawater and rust. Profits will not be enough to provide a great visitor experience *and* cover the cost of maintenance and upkeep.

For that reason, we are now well on our way to fully funding a $50-million USS *Midway* Foundation that will keep the great ship in peak condition in perpetuity so that visitors a century from now will continue to enjoy their visit as much as they do today.

When I look out my office window now and see that great ship berthed precisely at the spot I pointed out a quarter century ago, I couldn't be more proud or more excited. Part of that excitement comes from the knowledge that much of what has made the *Midway* successful are things we never saw coming. Unpredictable success is exhilarating, especially at my age. It means that the world can still show you something wonderful and new about the goodness of people.

CHAPTER 10

FAMILY AND TRAVEL

There is more to life than work.

That's easy to say, of course, but harder to believe—especially when the work is fulfilling, brings a degree of fame and reputation, and offers considerable material reward. It is even more difficult to step away from one's career when it is one of "good works"—when every day you see its positive impact on the lives of others, when there is a perpetual shortage of people who do what you do, and when the calls for help only grow over time.

And yet it is crucial that you never forget that there are others to whom you owe a different sort of duty of your time and commitment—your family, your friends, and ultimately yourself. I strongly believe that you cannot be a successful philanthropist, especially in the long term, if you have not fulfilled those other responsibilities. They ground you, give you perspective, and serve as the best possible lens through which to view the larger world. That's why, as we near the end of this narrative, I want to discuss this other side of my life and how it informs what I do in the nonprofit and charitable worlds.

Much of who we are is the result of events that took place long before we were born. Often, the circumstances by which we define ourselves and by which we are known are in fact the result of decisions made by others.

For example, I'm known as a native San Diegan. In fact, I'm often introduced that way, as if somehow I chose to grow up in my favorite city. The truth is that my father, Donald Burnham, grew up in Minnesota, and it wasn't until 1905, when he was eight, that *his* parents (my grandparents) decided to move to the Pacific coast and to the then-small town of San Diego.

By lucky coincidence my mother, Thelma, moved to San Diego at the same age and at the same time. Her parents had lived in Utah. Donald and Thelma met in high school and were married in their early twenties. They had two sons, my older brother Peter and me. Peter was born in 1926, and I came along in 1927. Peter succumbed to prostate cancer in 1993 at just sixty-seven.

I grew up in a middle-class family. We didn't have an especially large house or expensive furniture. Our one luxury, reflecting the times, was a full-time maid. She was a wonderful African American woman who took very good care of Peter and me. From our point of view, she had one extraordinary gift: she called us home for dinner with a whistle that seemed to carry for miles.

Our only other luxury was a nice little backyard. It had a line of guava trees, and every summer those trees would produce enough fruit to make guava jelly for the next twelve months. I can remember countless evenings eating dinner in the backyard with my father barbecuing hamburger steaks or swordfish on the grill.

We often idealize our childhoods, but mine was a remarkably happy one. I even enjoyed school. I went through the San Diego public school system—from kindergarten through sixth grade at Loma Portal School and then on to Point Loma High School, which in those days was a six-year program. In eleventh grade, I met my high school sweetheart; she would become my first wife. Most important of all, in terms of its lasting influence on my life, I learned how to sail in the waters of San Diego harbor, starting at age ten.

As I've already noted, I went to Stanford University and graduated in 1949, after four years, with a bachelor's degree in industrial engineering. The final summer was a busy one: in a matter of weeks I graduated, was married, and joined my father's firm. That's a lot of major events in a very brief period of time. It's a good thing youth is so resilient.

Three important ladies in my life:
my daughter, Cathe; stepmother, Esther; and wife, Roberta.

In May 1950, my wife presented us with twins: son John and daughter Cathleen, or "Cathe." As hard as it is sometimes for me to believe, John and Cathe are now sixty-five years old—senior citizens. It seems only yesterday that they were children running around the house.

Fourteen months later we had Tom, and MaryBeth, our fourth and last child, was born in 1955. Thus I recently became the father of four sexagenarians—a scenario I never could have imagined in those busy, thrilling, early days of parenthood.

Like all parents, I had specific guesses about what my kids would turn out to be in thirty or forty years. And like many parents, I missed those guesses by a mile. That's why I have no regrets about every second I spent with them as they were growing up. I traveled with them through every twist and turn of their young lives. I only regret that I didn't spend more time with them.

I missed the details, but not the substance of my expectations. My children have all grown into fine people. To my surprise at the time, none of them wanted to go into their father's business. I shouldn't have been surprised—after all, my brother didn't, either. Instead, my children grew into strong, independent people. Looking back, I shouldn't have asked for anything more.

Perhaps in part because of that same streak of independence, only John and Cathe have ever married. Cathe has given me my two grandchildren, Brian and Keith Jones. My prediction of eight grandchildren, like most such expectations, didn't pan out, but Brian and Keith filled my heart completely. In

May 2015, Keith and his wife Megan gave me my first great-granddaughter, Ella Grace.

Acquiring a sense of place perhaps even greater than my own, three of my children have chosen to stay and live in the San Diego area. John lives in Point Loma, just five minutes from our home. Cathe has a condo in La Jolla, and MaryBeth lives in the Julian area on Cuyamaca Mountain, about an hour from downtown San Diego. When my first wife and I divorced, Tom moved to be near her in Mendocino, and he still calls it home. It was the perfect place for him, as he and his mother share a strong artistic streak. Mendocino is on the Pacific coast about 150 miles north of San Francisco. Located in the wine country, it is known for its artistic residents and activities. Through the years, I've remained close to both Tom and his mother. All of us—including my wife Roberta—recently traveled up to Mendocino to be part of my ex-wife's funeral service.

My wife Roberta was born in Redlands, California. Like her parents and mine, Roberta went to work right out of high school, and she eventually moved to San Diego because her older sister was already there. She went to work at Bank of America and eventually became secretary to the manager at Bank of America's main office in downtown San Diego.

Roberta and I met in 1970. Both of us were going through divorces. A friend of mine felt sorry for me and invited me to a dinner party at his home. It was a very casual event on a Sunday evening, with fewer than a dozen people in the room, including a very lovely woman who had also come alone. Halfway through the party I went up to the host and asked about her: Was she his lady friend? "No, no," said my friend. "She's much too young for me. No, I wanted you to meet her."

So it seems I had unknowingly been part of a blind date—something I'd sworn I'd never do. As it turned out, that night proved to be the perfect introduction. Roberta met all of my prerequisites for my next wife: having been married before, not having children (as I had four already), and having worked. In addition, she has a great sense of humor and is very sensitive and empathetic. Roberta and I dated for a year and nine months. We were married in 1972 and have had a wonderful life together ever since.

One of the best things about having a close family is that it offers the opportunity to learn from each other. Because each of us does our own thing, we all have distinct experiences and skills we can share. My two daughters each had their own small businesses working out of their homes, both of them engaged with home decoration and refurbishing. That said, they operated in different worlds. Cathe was in higher-end properties such as luxury homes and commercial offices, and MaryBeth did smaller projects but was also in graphic arts. John, by comparison, spent his early work years in construction and development, working with an old associate of mine before branching out into property management and development. For the last two decades he has owned a very successful UPS store. Tom moved up to Mendocino to pursue his artistic talents, which include painting, drawing, clay sculpturing, theater, and landscaping. I can say without hesitation that all of my children have more people skills than I had at their age.

Another beautiful day of skiing Deer Valley Mountain in Utah.

My family is close, but we also have our own lives, and for that reason we've tried to create regular opportunities to spend time together. One way to do that is to take vacations together. For many years, we owned a condo in Deer Valley, Utah, that was large enough to hold all of us, and we spent many Christmases there together. We also have a place in Los Cabos, Baja Mexico, which is our current gathering place.

Needless to say, I've never really gotten sailing out of my system. In late 1987, when my days of climbing masts and pulling sheets were largely behind me, I swallowed hard and bought a ninety-foot, heavy-displacement, twin-diesel motor boat that we christened the *Bert & I*. Its four-thousand-mile cruising range essentially put the ports of the world within our reach, and we took full advantage of that capability. Looking at my travel diary for the following eleven years, I see that Roberta and I traveled more than 103,000 miles with 159 different guests, some joining us as many as six times.

Roberta and I have traveled the globe in three-week increments aboard our beloved boat, the Bert & I.

We spent nearly one-quarter of those eleven years—965 nights—on board *Bert & I*. It wasn't long before we developed a pattern of three-week adventures—to Florida, the East and West Coasts, the Caribbean, Fiji, the Galapagos, the Mediterranean, the South Pacific, and Alaska—featuring family for a week, guests for another week, and a week of private downtime for Roberta and me to "charge our batteries."

That wasn't our only traveling. We've found dry earth nearly as appealing as salt water. Largely as participants in Stanford University's wonderful international guided tour program, we have traveled to nearly every corner of the world on a total of fifteen trips. Our love for travel has hardly abated—as I edit these pages, we are on a National Geographic cruise of the islands of Indonesia.

You may well ask, if we have been traveling for perhaps a third of the last thirty years, how was I ever able to do my philanthropic work in San Diego? How could I manage all those boards, attend all those events, and oversee all those initiatives? My answer is that I don't think I could have been successful at all those things if I *hadn't* traveled.

I was born in San Diego, and I have lived here for nearly nine decades. That is a very long time, and it could have made my opinions and perspectives insular and shortsighted. As much as I love my city, I also recognize that there are other places, other cities, that have found their own solutions—some of which are better than ours. Travel taught me that. When I walk through the magnificent airport terminal in Singapore or sit drinking superb wine in a sidewalk café amid the crisp and efficient daily life of Cape Town, I am humbled by the realization that there is more than one way to do something well. We Americans, for all of our belief in our exceptionalism, haven't always found the best solutions. Travel opens my eyes to the great things happening in the world that I'd never otherwise know about.

If philanthropy is ultimately about trying to make and do things better, then travel is the best way to uncover some of the best practices of humankind. That process of discovery requires engagement. You can't learn enough about the world through the window of a tour bus or from the fourteenth floor of a luxury hotel. I remember walking through the airport terminal in Nairobi, Kenya, and being overwhelmed by all the banners strung throughout the place, as well as by the bandstands and flags that lined the road as we drove into the city.

I asked the driver what the occasion was for all of this celebration. He replied that Pope John Paul II was coming to Nairobi and that he would be riding along this road in the popemobile, which was being flown in for the visit.

In light of past events, I could hardly begrudge the Pope for traveling around in a bulletproof vehicle. But it also saddened me. How much could the head of the Roman Catholic Church really experience of his billion-member flock—particularly the poor and benighted of Africa—if he was driving by behind a wall of thick glass? I compared his experience with mine: crossing through the back country, sleeping in tents, having dinner with a local family and their goats in an igloo-like mud hut whose entrance tunnel I had to crawl through. His Holiness would only have encountered an artificial, scripted Kenya—one carefully prepared by his hosts. John Paul II only saw what they wanted him to see. As an unknown civilian, I got to see the real heart of Kenya and its wonderful, friendly, and creative people, and I took that knowledge back to my work in San Diego.

The Smart Border Coalition, an ongoing commitment of mine, has been deeply informed by my travel experiences. Living in San Diego, despite all of its interaction with Mexico, it is easy sometimes to forget that a foreign country—with different culture, history, and attitudes—lies just a few miles away. The Smart Border Coalition, which I cochair, has twelve board members from each side of the border. Officially, our task is to hire and advise the coalition's executive director and focus our efforts on making the border crossing more efficient for pedestrians, cars, and trucks. In reality, our task is far more sweeping and complex: we play an important role in the cultural exchange between the United States and Mexico as they interact along the western end of their common, two-thousand-mile-long border. Every day, we San Diego members of the coalition are reminded that we are not a stand-alone city: we are part of the largest multinational community in the entire world, with more than 6.5 million people. Our fates are intertwined, so we must find common ground and common cause.

It is with a vision of this mutual support that we created the coalition and other organizations like it. It is why I've been so supportive of the Kyoto Prize Symposium—especially its scholarship program for such worthy candidates as Rodrigo Ortega of Tijuana, whom I described in chapter 5. Had we not reached out across the border from both sides, a young man like Rodrigo might never have had the opportunity to accomplish what he has. And without my many travels, I would never have appreciated that there are many Rodrigos out there who need our support.

I will now move on to my final thought about family and philanthropy. As I've already noted, Roberta and I founded the Burnham Foundation in 1981 to map out and clarify what was then an improvised and scattershot pattern of donations to charitable causes. In fact, that was only half of our strategy. The other half was to begin exposing our children to the world of philanthropy, to educate them on its operation, and to start them on the road to becoming philanthropists themselves.

The first step was exposure. The then-new Burnham Foundation held regular board meetings, and we decided that in addition to me, Roberta, our estate attorney, tax people, and a general partner from my real estate investing, we would also rotate in one of our children. They would have no vote; instead, they would sit in and learn how we made decisions. I'm sure they sometimes found the process boring, but over the years—if only through osmosis—they picked up a lot of knowledge, and their interest grew.

Every five years or so, we made some revisions in our estate plan. One of the biggest occurred in 1995 when we set up the Burnham Family Foundation. Even after all these years, the Family Foundation still contains no assets, but after Roberta and I are gone, it will be the recipient of a major part of our estate. Our children are its four trustees. I think that they will thank us for preparing them for this enormous opportunity and challenge. We think that they will do a much better job with that money than they would by giving it to Uncle Sam in estate taxes.

In part because we were so careful and diligent about training them for this public role, all four of my children are now active in charitable giving—even sitting on the boards of some of those charities. I'd like to say that we planned all of this, but as parents we could only suggest and occasionally prod them into things they were already likely to do. Now that process is continuing into the next generation, with Brian and Keith following their parents' example.

All of this is hugely satisfying to me, not least because my children, grandchildren, and great-grandchild are happy and healthy but also because I know that at least to a small degree they have followed me down my path, as I followed my father's. I know that the Burnham tradition of good citizenship is likely to continue well into this century.

It is this idea of legacy to which I will now devote my final chapter.

CHAPTER 11

LEGACY

I have devoted most of this book to talking about the past. I'd like to use this final chapter to discuss the future.

The notion of the *future* and our place within it necessarily changes over time. When I was a young man, newly married and starting my career, the future was the place where I would play out my career and, with luck and hard work, perhaps make my mark. It was where, if everything went right, I might find a measure of success and satisfaction.

I write this at age eighty-eight, living in a twenty-first-century world I never could have imagined in the middle of the twentieth century. The future is a very different place. The odds are that I won't get to see much more of it. I am as busy now as I ever was, but I find that I now ponder more about the mark I will leave in this world and the nature of its importance—or the lack thereof.

The notion of *legacy* is a complex one. Too often, it is the obsession of men and women at the end of their careers as they scramble to polish their reputations and cover their tracks before it is too late. Sometimes they succeed, but more often than not, the nature of their reputations is out of their control and will be decided by others in the years to come. And those final reputations, created after the polish and gilding have worn away, are usually quite fair and just.

If there is one truth that people should live by, it is that they should start thinking about their legacy at the *beginning* of their careers—when they are taking the actions, good or bad, that will make their reputations—rather than at the end, when it is too late.

This is yet another reason to get involved with philanthropy early in one's career rather than at the end. Philanthropy offers a way to leave a positive legacy and, if started early, can make that legacy a more consequential one. Just as important, devoting a sizable portion of one's life to good works is itself a disciplining process: it teaches perspective, empathy, and priority. When you sit on the board of an organization that helps the poor and disadvantaged, you cannot escape the reality of that world, you can't hide from its ugly truths, and you can't help but feel a duty to help. It may not make you a better person (though it probably will), but it will make you a better-behaved person, a better citizen, and a better neighbor.

By the same token, if your philanthropy runs to civic development, your participation will teach you that your community is not just the people you know or the members of your economic or social class but *all* of its residents. Whether they are rich or poor, natives or newly arrived, young or old, they all deserve a voice in determining the future of the place they call home.

If your philanthropy is in scientific research, you are humbled by the realization that you are investing in solutions that may appear long after you are gone and that you are trusting the fate of your money to people who are often far smarter than you, working on arcane problems about which you may have limited understanding.

In other words, as much as it may appear to outsiders as a role of prestige, power, and influence, philanthropy is often a role defined by humility, powerlessness, and lack of control. After a half century, I see that this is a good thing. When you run a business, you are in charge; you can order your subordinates to follow your strategy or risk their jobs, and success and failure can be measured on a balance sheet.

Philanthropy is infinitely more subtle. When you sit on the board of a charity or nonprofit, you have little control beyond the selection of its chief executive; you can only motivate, not tell, volunteers to give their time and talent; and most of all, success and failure are elusive terms with no accurate yardstick to measure them. This alternative reality can be very difficult for business executives accustomed to command-and-control organizations to accept. Until they learn their limitations in this new world, they can often be very destructive without ever knowing why.

I'd like to say that I escaped these traps, but it isn't true. When I first left the commercial world for philanthropy, I too was a bit of a bull in a china shop with the first organizations I helped. But I learned over time—yet another reason for starting early.

The hard truth about legacies is that by definition, we don't get to see them play out. We can only hope that future generations will think well of us, and we can't correct any mistakes or misperceptions. On the one hand, that can be liberating: if the future of our reputation is out of our control, then why worry too much about it? On the other hand, it is frightening: if we have devoted our lives to building or supporting institutions that we want to make a positive impact on the world in future generations, shouldn't we make every effort to make sure that those institutions endure?

Resolving that apparent contradiction isn't simple. To my mind, the only way to do so is to continue to work as hard as you can to make those institutions, initiatives, and programs that you believe in strong enough, resilient enough, and sufficiently well managed to endure whatever challenges the future throws at them. If you can raise your children and help raise your grandchildren to lead those efforts after you are gone and to reflect your philosophy, so much the better. Beyond that, it is out of your hands, so why worry about something beyond your control? Trust instead in the basic goodness of human beings. No one is irreplaceable; somewhere out there is the person who will take your place. Leave them a good record of what you've done so they can learn from your example.

Looking back, the first time I helped to create a legacy was when I was still in the commercial world—and I did so largely unconsciously. At John Burnham Real Estate under my father, and later at Burnham Real Estate Services under my leadership, we had a wonderful family atmosphere. We all called ourselves "associates," and we not only worked together but also played together after work. So strong was this family culture that even after the firm was sold to Cushman & Wakefield, there remained at our old offices what came to be called "the Burnham Spirit."

Forty years later, that spirit has evolved and adapted to changing times, but it is still true to its core. Our insurance company spin-off still presents a "Spirit of Burnham" award. I have no doubt that it will go out of style eventually, as our family name disappears from the employees' memory, but I am also certain that some germ of that old spirit will continue to define the company for as long as it exists. And that—not least because it is a tribute as much to my father as to me—is deeply satisfying.

Another example of legacy-as-culture in my life is the Sanford Burnham Prebys Medical Discovery Institute. I'm far less concerned about how long my name is attached to the Institute than I am that the DNA of collaboration that defines it and makes it special is never diluted by time. However the institute grows and whatever new lines of research it pursues, as long as future generations of scientists there maintain that collaborative culture, the institute will remain a major force for good.

Equally important to me is the San Diego Foundation (SDF) and with it the Center for Civic Engagement. It means a great deal to me not just because I was there at its founding, helped build it along the way, and then had the inspiration for the physical center itself, but because it can be a powerful force for good. The $850 million the SDF has distributed to the San Diego community has profoundly changed the lives of hundreds of thousands of people. And with the Center for

Civic Engagement, we've taken the next step: not just helping people but giving them, whatever their station, a real voice in the future of their city. Someday they'll remove my name from above the door, but if the SDF is still on a strong financial footing and the Center is a vibrant part of the city's strategic planning, I won't mind at all.

Lecturing my friend, Senator Pete Wilson, in 1983,
in front of a packed audience. Wilson would go on to become Governor.

As for who will sit in my chair at all those board meetings across the city, I don't flatter myself that no else can do my job. People sat on those seats before I arrived, and I don't doubt they will still be warm when my replacements sit in them.

One of the great things about living and working in a large city like San Diego is that there is no shortage of smart, successful people who want to pay back some of their good luck and are willing to pitch in to help when asked. Thirty years ago, when future California Governor Pete Wilson was our mayor, he labeled San Diego "America's Finest City." I still agree with that moniker, though I think it has become a bit stale. These days I'm stumping for a more ambitious description: "The Miracle Coast," running from Baja California to Santa Monica. After all, think of all of the miracles we have performed here in recent years—from genome sequencing to the world's leadership in drones to great new companies like Qualcomm—as well as a superb quality of life, a vibrant relationship with the nation next door, and an urban infrastructure of unmatched quality. What other city can boast all that?

Do I sound like a booster? You bet. But I'm also not alone. My city is filled with talented, enthusiastic people who are just as dedicated as I am to San Diego's future. That's why I'm not worried about who will replace me; I have no doubt that they'll be even more effective than me.

Here is a big part of my real legacy—my family—gathered around Roberta and me during my eightieth birthday aboard the USS Midway Museum.

From left to right: my daughter, Cathe; granddaughter-in-law, Megan; grandson, Keith; grandson, Brian; daughter, MaryBeth; son, Tom; stepmother, Esther; and son, John.

I'll even predict that one of those stellar figures will be a part of the Burnham family. My grandson Keith Jones has already shown the aptitude to take the torch and carry on my legacy in the nonprofit world. I hope he does, but whatever great things he accomplishes will be part of his legacy, not mine. My work is still here and now, and I can't dictate the long-term future.

My other grandson, Brian Jones, has recently returned to San Diego after some twenty plus years pursuing his education followed by a variety of other endeavors. He is on the gregarious side with multiple talents which should bode him well. It is no surprise that he has joined a national real estate development firm with an office in San Diego.

The older I get, the more I realize that a person's real legacy is not the buildings that bear their name or the money they've given away to good causes but the impact they leave on the hearts of others. A shiny new building bearing your name can be an impressive thing, but your greatest impact may come instead from the few words you say to someone during a critical time in his or her life. Your words can change someone's life's trajectory—and as a result, that person in turn can change the world around him or her.

I've just listed some of what I think are my *institutional* legacies. Time will tell just what impact I may have had on all those charities and nonprofits to which I dedicated my energies. I also like to think that I will leave behind some *personal* legacies—pieces of my personality and style that have had an impact on others. Some may have lasted only seconds; some, I hope, will last a lifetime.

I present these to you humbly, knowing that in some cases I may be overestimating myself (and in others underestimating myself) and that those who know me well might disagree with some of the entries on the list.

1. *I try to put community before self.* If the success and health of your community is your highest goal, more than your own self-interest, you will have no trouble finding help. Your motives will never be suspect. Your engagement with something larger than yourself will act as a compass in keeping you on the right path.

2. *I endeavor to be a team player.* It's simple mathematics: the more talented people you can bring together to solve a problem—especially if they are of diverse backgrounds and skills—the greater your chance to find the best solution. Of course, that also means you must devote considerable energy to working with others, even if they are very different from you. Start by getting your ego out of the way.

3. *I cultivate multiple interests.* Teamwork is not just a diversity of players but also a diversity of interests in your own life. The more interests you have, the more wisdom you are likely to bring to any project.

4. *If I throw out many ideas, some will stick.* Once again, this is about ego. Too often people toss out their best idea and fight for it against every alternative.

But brainstorming isn't a contest. Having your idea "win" at all costs almost never helps the organization. The secret to success lies in getting *every* idea out there and then choosing the best one, regardless of its author.

5. *I believe that variety beats total focus.* Focus is good. Focus brings our intelligence and experience to bear on the task at hand. But focus can often lead to tunnel vision, a restricted tool kit, and a lack of perspective on what actually constitutes a successful result. That's why, unlike many of my peers, I've never focused on one or two charities or subjects for my philanthropy. Instead, I engage them across a broad spectrum in the belief that any cross-fertilization I bring to each will be an advantage.

6. *I fight to keep my ego under control.* When you are successful, it's hard not to have a big ego, even when you know it is ultimately a disadvantage. The key, I think, is not to tell yourself to be modest but rather to accept that you have an ego and to regularly remind yourself to keep it under control. One way to do that is to consciously make yourself the best team player possible. Another strategy, once again, is to put the needs of the organization and your community ahead of your own.

7. *I hope to be generally an "open book."* One of the biggest challenges to being a successful public figure is that it multiplies the demands placed upon your

time. Saying no is hard, especially when so many people and institutions seem so worthy. It's much easier to install filters—unlisted phone numbers, secretaries and receptionists, a gated community, a car and driver—to keep from ever having to say no. As difficult as it's been over the years, I've fought to keep myself accessible, even to the point of keeping my phone number listed. You'd be surprised how easily you adapt to this openness and to the number of important opportunities you would have missed otherwise.

8. *I try to let everybody participate.* If your effectiveness grows with the number and diversity of people you team up with, then it stands to reason that you want to be as inclusive as possible. We all have a tendency to join with people who are most like us, who have the same level of education, class, lifestyle, age, gender, and so on. Left to our own prejudices, we will do just that. I'm hardly exempt from that bias. The key, for me at least, has been to consciously force myself to reach out to all potential stakeholders in a project. If I do, I know that everyone's voice will be heard.

9. *I give away responsibility and authority.* I'd like to claim that I naturally distribute leadership as a matter of a personal philosophy. But the fact is that I learned to do so largely because I was forced into it by circumstances. At the beginning of my career

as a philanthropist, I joined so many different boards of directors that I simply didn't have time to do everything myself, even when I wanted to. As a result, largely by default, I learned the power of assigning duties to others and empowering them to do the jobs themselves. The final step did fit with my personality: give credit where it's due—to the people who did the work.

10. *I'm willing to accept failure and try to learn from it.* It's become almost a cliché in the high-tech business world that failure can be a good thing. It disciplines entrepreneurs, refines products, and pioneers new and unknown markets. Unfortunately, that philosophy has never really penetrated the world of nonprofits. Perhaps it's because failure in the business world is seen as merely about money and jobs, while with charities it is seen as a matter of life and death. The truth is that the risk is rarely that dire. And without accepting risk and the potential for a "good" failure, charities, research laboratories, and social enterprises can never *learn.* They can't get better at what they do, and they can't evolve. If I'm not taking a risk, I worry that I'm doing something wrong.

11. *I keep my commitments, even if it's costly to do so.* It isn't enough to say that you're willing to accept failure; you have to live it as well. The old saying that "success has a thousand fathers, while failure is an orphan" is unfortunately proven every day in

the nonprofit world. But the reality is that each time you run from failure—or worse, shift the blame to someone else—you lose a piece, large or small, out of your reputation for integrity, and for being a stand-up person. People will trust you less the next time, and you will become increasingly risk-averse with each new project. The years have taught me that it is far better to bite the bullet and fail—and to accept the cost of that failure. For one thing, you will lose some of your fear of failure. For another, rather than diminishing you in the eyes of others, they will see you as a person of integrity—as someone they can trust.

12. *I'm a good cheerleader.* Never underestimate the power of enthusiasm. When your team is happy and engaged, it can accomplish prodigious things that are impossible for a grim-faced group. I've learned that *cheerleading* is not simply the act of putting a smile on your face and rah-rahing your team. Rather, it is actually a medium of engagement. The team coalesces around your positive attitude, which reinforces the team members' sense of their own value and purpose and carries you through the inevitable rough spots.

13. *I accept change and attempt to look around corners.* It is a myth that the older you become, the more resistant you are to change. That may be true for some people, but I could introduce you to a number of men and women in their seventies and eighties who are

ferocious risk takers and who embrace change. I like to think that I'm one of them. Why are older people still risk takers? Because we have seen more change than our younger counterparts and have a stronger sense of its inevitability. We know that time is short, and we have less to lose. The truth is that once you break your attachment to the status quo, you gain greater vision into the future—not least because you can face the implications of today's trends fearlessly and honestly.

14. *I work to be a consensus builder.* As I noted earlier in this book, managing a charity or nonprofit requires a different management style than the commercial, for-profit sector. In the latter, you motivate mostly by salary, title, and other measurable incentives. By comparison, people in the nonprofit world—from volunteers to employees to board members—devote their time and energy for more intangible reasons: helping others, feeling that their contributions matter, and fulfilling a personal moral imperative. In other words, they don't *have* to do this work; indeed, they usually could make more money working for a corporation. So you cannot motivate these folks via executive fiat or threats to their careers. Rather, you must build consensus. You must create a context in which they *choose* to follow where you want to lead them. That is something many business executives have trouble learning when they cross over into

nonprofits. I too have had to learn by trial and error. The good news is that once you've built this consensus, you get to lead the most motivated and loyal team imaginable.

15. *I am a door opener.* I've chosen to be the guy who is not afraid to talk with anyone and to enlist them into the latest community endeavor—the person who is willing and unafraid to ask for money. I've tried to be the guy who can open doors. Once again, I pretty much fell into this role by default. As a realtor, I learned early on that success goes to the gregarious, to the person who is not afraid to talk money and close the deal. Just as important, from the start I knew that though our foundation was meaningful, I was never going to be in the same league, even in San Diego, as some of the big philanthropic titans. I would never come close to operating at the same level as, say, John D. Spreckels earlier in the century. If I was going to have a real impact, I knew that I would have to seed my projects with the initial money and then go out and find powerful associates, even if it meant putting their name before mine on the resulting institution. As you've seen, that was the story of the Sanford Burnham Prebys Medical Discovery Institute. As a strategy to create the maximum leverage, I can't recommend it enough—though be prepared to keep your ego in check.

Will the future remember me as all of these things? Probably not. Like every other philanthropist, in the end I can only hope that these bits and pieces of who I am and what I've done endure at least for a while and perhaps survive in the personalities of others who follow me. And if, in time, my name disappears from the entrances and facades of buildings—and eventually even from documents and official histories—it doesn't matter, as long as the good works themselves endure. Because in the end, that's what it was all about.

As I near the end of my career, I often look back in wonder. I was born at the right time, into a happy and loving family and a wonderful city on the cusp of historic expansion. I was blessed to be part of that emerging, dynamic region. Sometimes I was in the lead, sometimes in the caboose, and sometimes in the middle. But I was always part of a team; I accomplished nothing by myself. So to all of my teammates over the decades, I am eternally grateful. Together we helped turn a small Navy port in a distant corner of the nation into one of the largest and most important business, tourist, and military centers on the planet.

These days, I don't sail as much as I used to. When I do, I once again become that little ten-year-old boy navigating his tiny sailboat out into the great harbor. When I look back on the mighty skyline of my hometown, I can still see, beneath the skyscrapers, the great ships, and the stadium, the San Diego that was, that is, and that will be. I am humbled by the sight, by the fact that I was given the chance to be part of that history for longer than I ever could have imagined and that I'm still part of that story.

And I think what a lucky guy I am.

MALIN BURNHAM'S BEACONS

Over the years, I've developed a list of personal rules. I call them "beacons" because they act as guides and warnings, and they illuminate the correct path ahead to help me deal with career (and even personal) challenges. I've discussed many of these in the text, but there are others you may find just as useful.

1. Change will happen; anticipate and take advantage of it.
2. Lead, follow, or get out of the way.
3. Concentrate on the team and *we*, rather than *I*.
4. Hard work gets better results.
5. The goal should be self-confidence, not self-congratulation.
6. Prioritize and use a "to-do list."
7. Don't forget to thank people.
8. Live a balanced life with a healthy diet, exercise, travel, reading, and many friends.
9. Get out of your rut; consider re-potting yourself.
10. Don't tell people what to do; only give them ideas.
11. Ethics is all about doing the right thing.

12. There are many benefits to taking time off to "recharge our batteries."

13. When delegating responsibility, it's best to give authority as well.

14. Don't suffer from failure; after all, you are one step closer to success.

15. It's easy to be a philanthropist: you can make a gift, ask for the gift, or volunteer your time and energy.

16. Be prepared to lead, even if you are not in charge.

THE VIRTUES OF EXCELLENCE

Every person with whom I work eventually encounters my underlying philosophy of being a successful person and professional. While it is implicit in everything I do, I like to make this list of virtues explicit whenever possible to fellow board members, teammates, and recipients of my philanthropic efforts. As you can see, each combines an overarching philosophical statement with its real-world execution.

Plan Ahead: Set personal goals. Adjust them with time and circumstance.

Commitment: Take responsibility for your words and deeds. Fulfill your promises.

Hard Work: Put in the time and energy to fulfill your commitments. Be prepared—not only schedule the necessary time, but be prepared and work intelligently to use that time efficiently.

Dedication: Never give up. Success often comes when you think it is no longer possible.

Teamwork: Everyone has something to contribute, so treat everyone fairly, and share credit for every success.

Play by the Rules: Be honest, ethical, and fair. If your project is worthy of success, it is also worthy of being done right. Cutting corners will always come back to punish you.

Follow Through: Never trust luck to achieve your goals. Take positive action toward success, and be unrelenting until that success is achieved. Never coast to the finish line—you may never get there.

MALIN BURNHAM

One of the virtues of starting early and living long is that it offers a wonderful opportunity to be involved in a lot of exciting projects—and to see their successful conclusion. Though I find it hard to believe, at last count, during my thirty-seven year business career, I cofounded and chaired three firms that became listed on the New York and American stock exchanges. In total, I've been a board member and/or officer of eighteen business corporations and thirty-two nonprofit organizations. And I've loved every day of it.